1-50

THE FLAME OF FREEDOM

by the same author

A Fearful Freedom

THE FLAME OF FREEDOM

*Corporal Ras Pagani's escape
from the Railway of Death*

by

ROBERT HAMOND

These things shall be! A loftier race
Than e'er the world hath known, shall rise
With flame of freedom in their souls
And light of knowledge in their eyes.

*New and Old. A Vista
John Addington Symonds*

**LEO COOPER
LONDON**

First published 1988 by Leo Cooper Ltd
Leo Cooper is an independent imprint of
the Heinemann Group of Publishers,
10 Upper Grosvenor Street, London W1X 9PA

LONDON MELBOURNE JOHANNESBURG AUCKLAND

ISBN 0–85052–2862

Photoset in Great Britain by
Deltatype Lecru, Ellesmere Port, Cheshire
and printed by Biddles Ltd, Guildford and King's Lynn

DEDICATION

To Major Hugh Paul Seagrim GC, DSO, MBE,
and to the Karen people who suffered and died in the
defence of their freedom, 1942–1945.

CONTENTS

ILLUSTRATIONS

20. An NCO of the Kempeitai (copyright © 1986 Ronald Searle)
21. Pagani in 1987.

The author and publishers are grateful to the following for permission to reproduce copyright illustrations: R.A.S. Pagani, Nos. 1, 2, 3, 17 and 21; Lt-Col J.H. Seagrim, No. 4; E.J. Wright, Esq, No. 5; Messrs Faber & Faber, Nos. 6, 8, 9, 10, 12, 13, 14, 15, 16 and 18; Father Jean Verinaud, Archiviste, Missions Etrangères de Paris, Nos 7 and 11; M. Louis Calmon, No. 19; The Imperial War Museum, No. 20.

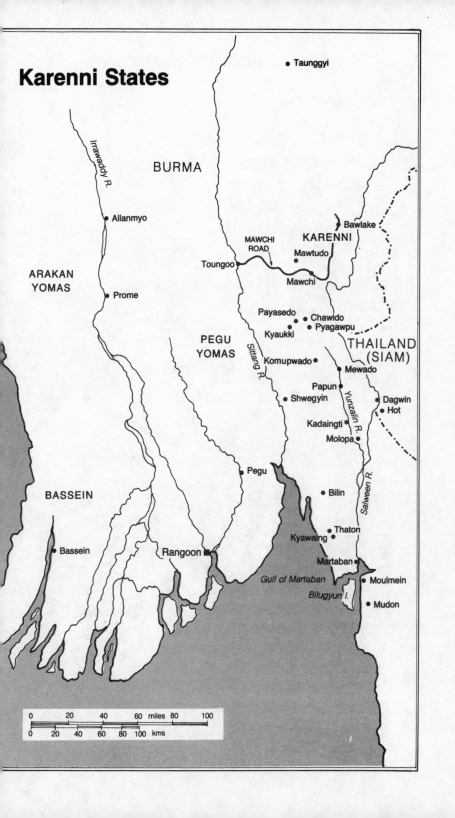

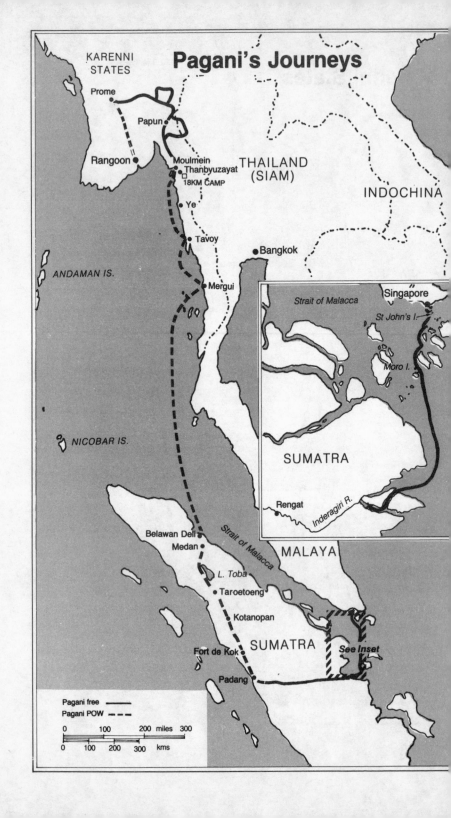

Pagani's Journeys

KARENNI
STATES

Prome

Papun

Rangoon

Moulmein
Thanbyuzayat
18KM CAMP

THAILAND
(SIAM)

INDOCHINA

Ye

Tavoy

Bangkok

ANDAMAN IS.

Mergui

Singapore

Strait of Malacca

St John's I.

Moro I.

NICOBAR IS.

SUMATRA

Rengat

Inderagiri R.

Belawan Deli

Medan

Strait of Malacca

MALAYA

L. Toba

Taroetoeng

Kotanopan

SUMATRA

Fort de Kok

See Inset

Padang

Pagani free ———
Pagani POW – – –

0   100   200 miles 300

0   100   200   300   kms

GLOSSARY

BIA	Burma Independence Army (pro-Japanese).
Changkul	Tool used in Asia for digging/hoeing ground.
Dah	Jungle slashing knife.
Dāl	Lentils.
Kempeitai	Japanese security police like German *Gestapo*.
Naik	Corporal (Indian Army).
Oozie	Elephant driver.
Padi	Rice fields.
Pagoda	Buddhist temple.
Pāgri	Turban (Indian).
Pongyi	Buddhist monk/priest.
Sampan	Small boat.
Saw	Title of all male Karens – 'Mr' (*Naw* all female Karens – 'Mrs/Miss') Karens from Mission Schools often took English names, some very original.
Tenko	Roll call parade (Japanese).
Topee	Pith helmet.
Towkay	Chinese merchant.
Yomas	Mountains/mountain ranges (Burmese).

PRONUNCIATIONS – BURMESE

au pronounced ow
gyi pronounced jee
kyi pronounced chee
Karen pronounced Karēn
Papun pronounced Parpoon
Kyaukki pronounced Chowkchee
Pyagawpu pronounced Pee-yag-apoo

yin pronounced jin
gyaw pronounced jaw
kyaw pronounced chaw

AUTHOR'S NOTE

In 1978, while I was researching my book, *A Fearful Freedom*, I came across a diary which the late Major D. P. Apthorp, M.B.E., The Royal Norfolk Regiment, had kept, secretly, whilst a prisoner of the Japanese, 1942–1945.

The diary for the period March, 1942–January, 1944, he buried in 18 Km camp, South Burma, hoping to retrieve it after the war. However, he was unable to return there so he re-wrote it after his return to England in 1945 and placed a copy in the archives of his Regiment. Here it remained for over thirty years, unread as far as I know, by officers or men of the Regiment who had been taken prisoner at Singapore, and many of whom had laboured on the notorious Burma-Siam railway where the only certain escape was in death from overwork, brutal treatment, starvation and disease.

The diary was in great detail and contained Nominal Rolls of the British Officers and men of many regiments, who had escaped from Singapore to Sumatra but had later been captured while they waited, in vain, for ships to come and take them to safety.

The Japanese later shipped this party – known as the British (Sumatra) Battalion – to southern Burma. Here they were put to work on building the railway eastwards towards Siam. Other prisoners of war, including myself, were brought from Singapore by train to Siam and constructed the railway westwards towards Burma, through the jungles of Siam.

As I read through the diary, reliving the all-too-familiar descriptions of disease, misery and death, I suddenly came across a paragraph which brought my reading to an abrupt halt.

'It was about this time that (Corporal) Pagani, 18 Division Reconnaissance Regiment, escaped. He left 18 Kilo camp at the end of November (1942) and was not heard of again until he arrived in England in June, 1945.'

I found this an astounding piece of information. To the best of my knowledge no one had made a successful escape from the railway. Those who tried were usually betrayed to the Japanese by local people to claim the reward which the Japanese had put on the head of any escaping prisoner. After recapture, escapers were returned to their camps, brutally treated and then shot or bayoneted. A lucky few were given over to the sadistic care of the *Kempeitai* 'for special treatment'. Some of these, after enduring unspeakable brutalities and privations, lived to tell the tale, although with greatly impaired health.

This paragraph implied that Pagani had made a successful escape – almost certainly the only one from the railway. Otherwise, why was he not returned to his camp for execution and how did he get home in June, 1945, some four months ahead of other PoWs in the railway camps?

While I pondered the matter there swam up out of the depths of my memory a casual remark which I had heard in one of the camps, over thirty years earlier, that the only

man who had escaped from the railway in Burma had been
a Eurasian medical orderly, who spoke Hindustani and was
able to pass as an Indian. While this seemed remotely
possible I thought no more about it at the time as the camps
were full of strange tales and rumours, many of them
without any foundation at all, but useful for boosting
morale.

Now I see that Pagani was the man; his description of
himself as 'a European mongrel' could easily have been
corrupted into 'Eurasian' and, during the writing of his
story, I have found that he had been working in the camp
hospital until shortly before his escape.

Several months of detective work followed before I
found Pagani. At first he seemed reluctant to tell his story
to a stranger and, as I was busy writing *A Fearful Freedom*, I
let the matter rest.

Two years later I decided to go and see him at his home
in Clacton-on-Sea.

During our conversations I found that we had many
interests in common – service in India, a love of the
countryside and a knowledge of the Himalayas. I also
learned more about Pagani himself and was able to form
my own opinion of him.

I saw him as a man of great determination, courage and
resource who had made his escape plans and dared to
carry them out alone. His urge to get back into the war
had driven him on relentlessly, over-riding the sure
knowledge that failure would almost certainly result in
execution by the Japanese, and discounting the tremendous odds stacked against a white man, already to some
extent debilitated by months of inadequate diet and
native diseases, and without the essential escape aids of
food, medicine, maps or compass. He had deliberately set
himself the seemingly impossible task of travelling on foot

through hundreds of miles of country, inhabited (he had to assume) by natives who were not only hostile but willing to betray him to the Japanese for reward.

That he failed, at the eleventh hour, to complete what would have been one of the most daring escapes of all time does not detract from the fact that he was far more successful in his attempt than anyone else in that theatre of war.

Of course he had luck; luck that his frail *sampan* was not overwhelmed in the storm off Sumatra; luck that the Indians of southern Burma had been so persecuted by the pro-Japanese Burma Independent Army that they were willing to guide and conceal him; luck that not only did he have a fair knowledge of Hindustani but that his French was fluent and later enabled him to make himself understood to the French missionaries in the Karenni States.

Without such strokes of fortune his escapes would have ended in disaster at an early stage and he would have died or been killed. But he also had some bad luck, his separation from his faithful guide, Lance Naik Mura, and his failure to find a boat in which to cross the Irrawaddy river being the worst.

However, even in such moments of great peril, he was saved by his quick wits and his resource. Perhaps only those who were themselves prisoners of the Japanese, and witnessed the cruelties which they inflicted on recaptured prisoners before execution, can appreciate fully the ghastly risks which Pagani was willing to take.

They will salute him for the way in which he constantly challenged fortune and for which he was awarded a well-deserved Military Medal.

Robert Hamond

PREFACE

Roy Anthony Stephen Pagani was born at 2.15 am on 23 July, 1915, at Fulham, London. His grandfather was Italian and his grandmother English, the former working for 25 years as restaurant manager at the Grosvenor Hotel, London. His father was English and his mother French.

When he was four years old, and his sister two, his parents separated, his mother remaining in London and his father taking the two children to Paris where he had business interests. They spent every winter on the Riviera and, eventually, their father returned to Paris leaving them at Cannes in the care of his mistress. Before long she eloped with another man, abandoning the children. Their father did not return to claim them – in fact, they never saw him again – so they were taken in as orphans by a Convent of mixed sexes at Cannes. Young Roy managed to get in touch with his mother who assumed responsibility for them, sending money so that the children could be educated.

At the age of ten Roy went on to a 'boys only' Convent

boarding school, just outside Toulon, The Institution of St Joseph, La Navarre, in the little village of La Crau.

This was an unusual school; in addition to conventional education, the staff encouraged the boys to become resourceful and self-sufficient. The school had stock farms, vineyards and vegetable gardens on which staff and pupils worked as part of their training to fit them for life after leaving school. At weekends they made expeditions into the neighbouring hills to hunt wild boar and deer, or to fish and collect mushrooms and other wild fruits and vegetables. No practical aspect of life was neglected; they collected insects and flowers for study in their nature classes and were taught to recognize the stars at night.

In the school religious instruction formed a vital part of their education; their food and their language was entirely French. Their most important game on the playground was called *Le Drapeau*, a team game in which individuals had to break through the opposing team to reach a flag hanging at the end of the playground.

These country pursuits turned Roy into a knowledgeable and practical countryman and the challenge of *Le Drapeau* instilled in him a burning determination to be dominant in anything to which he set his hand.

Apart from visits to his mother each Christmas, Roy remained at the school until he was over thirteen years old. He had been very happy there, had developed a great love of France and spoke and thought like any French boy.

He then returned to his mother whom he begged not to send him to an English school where he would be at a great disadvantage due to his lack of English. She agreed, so he began to look for work.

Although he was obviously under-age, potential

employers turned a blind eye and at last he was successful in being taken on as page-boy at the Victoria Hotel in Northumberland Avenue, dressed in a pill-box hat and smart multi-buttoned jacket and trousers. Until he was seventeen and a half years old he worked at various jobs in several hotels, finishing up at the Park Lane Hotel.

In July, 1933, on one afternoon off, he went for a bicycle ride. He passed the Depot, of The East Surrey Regiment, at Kingston on Thames, and then stopped. Perhaps I'm fit enough to join the Army, he mused; I'll give it a try. He went in and said that he wished to join the Army. He was welcomed because recruiting was very slow at that time due to memories of the horrors of war in the trenches in the Great War. After a medical check he was measured for height. He was only 5′ 5″ so the recruiting sergeant said, 'Can't you get a bit higher? Your heels are very heavy on the ground?' Roy raised his heels a little and was instantly accepted.

After signing on the dotted line he was given some pay and told to report back in a week.

At first he did not know how to break the news to his mother but eventually he confessed that he had joined the Army. She stared at him for a long moment.

'You're a fool,' she replied. 'You could have gone as an officer.'

'I don't want to be an officer,' he protested. 'I want to be like everyone else.'

There was no further argument, although his mother was far from happy about his action. The following week he started his training, which lasted six months, after which he was posted to the 2nd Battalion at Shorncliffe.

In 1934 he went with a draft to the 1st Battalion, which was stationed at Faizabad in India, where he remained until 1937. This proved to be a useful experience as, apart from becoming a trained soldier, he had the opportunity of observing Indians, a factor which was to stand him in good stead in his escapes during the coming war.

The 1st Battalion sailed for Khartoum late in 1937 and returned to England in January, 1939. Roy Pagani got married in Colchester in August, 1939, and was training in Southern England when war was declared.

In October the Battalion sailed for France where Roy felt very much at home. His fluent French made him invaluable as an interpreter and he enjoyed every moment of the 'phoney war'.

On 10 May, 1940, the Germans began their invasion of Holland and Belgium and, for the next three weeks, the East Surreys conducted a fighting withdrawal to Dunkirk. Their story, as with the gallant fighting retreats of so many County Regiments, has been recorded in detail elsewhere and has no further place in this narrative. Suffice it to say that, bombed and machine-gunned incessantly, and utterly exhausted, the remnants of the Battalion at last embarked at Dunkirk and reached Dover safely on 1 June. They had lost all their vehicles and heavy equipment; twelve officers and 259 men had been killed, wounded or were missing.

Roy Pagani was among the survivors. Two thoughts dominated his mind as he sank gratefully to sleep in safety for the first time in weeks; firstly, he had seen that the training, strength and equipment of the British Army was no match for the German Army at this time and, secondly, due to his French upbringing, he had developed a fierce hatred for the Germans whom he had seen so ruthlessly trampling on the country and people he loved. He was determined to get back into action against the enemy as soon as possible.

But England was now under seige. Most units were totally occupied in reforming, re-equipping and taking up static defensive positions to repel a likely invasion by the Germans. There seemed little opportunity of fighting them unless they were to land in England, and Pagani got the impression that such training as they were able to carry out was a continuation of the tactics which had already proved inadequate against superior German tactics.

He therefore decided to volunteer for any unit which gave promise of action. His application to join the Parachute Regiment failed, as did his bid to join the Commandos. He applied to go to the newly-formed Reconnaissance Corps and was accepted. Eventually he was posted to 18 Reconnaissance Battalion which was part of the ill-fated 18th Division. This battalion had been formed from the 5th Battalion, The Loyal Regiment and, among these Territorial soldiers, Pagani was respected as a man with experience of war and nicknamed 'Ras' by his comrades on account of his initials.

18th Division sailed at the end of October, 1941, bound for Egypt, and Ras looked forward to this opportunity of avenging the defeat of his beloved France. However, the entry of Japan into the war diverted the Division, first to India for about two weeks, and then to Singapore.

18 Reconnaissance Battalion, in the *Empress of Asia*, had been at sea for nearly three months under cramped conditions which had made them physically soft and had inevitably blunted the cohesion which is so vital to troops about to be committed to battle. Apart from these disadvantages, the long voyage had been uneventful and even pleasant. As they passed through the Sunda Strait on 3 February, a few days from Singapore, the jungle-

covered hills on either side of the Strait evoked mild interest and held no obvious menace.

They were, however, soon to be rudely awakened and Corporal Ras Pagani was to achieve his ambition to get back into the fighting, although not in the way he had intended.

On 4 February they were approaching the Banka Strait, the *Empress of Asia* leading the convoy, when they heard the sound of aircraft and soon spotted a formation of high-flying Japanese bombers. These released their bombs at a given command and, although there were no direct hits or major damage to the convoy, several bombs fell near the *Empress of Asia*. Splinters holed her boats and rafts and the stokers abandoned the engine room in panic. Eventually they were ordered below again but by now the ship had fallen astern of the convoy.

During the following morning, as they turned on the last ten-mile leg to Singapore docks, five enemy dive-bombers attacked them, scoring three direct hits, one of which went down the funnel and set the ship on fire amidships. After dropping their bombs, the planes attacked for half an hour with machine-guns, in spite of heavy fire from the escorting naval vessels.

The *Empress of Asia* began to list and the fires to spread. She was obviously doomed and orders were given to abandon ship. *HMAS Yarra* came alongside and her Australian captain emphasized the urgency with some very colourful language. The evacuation of the ship was carried out in a calm manner controlled by Lieutenant-Colonel Fitt, who was later awarded the DSO for his conduct in such dangerous circumstances. Men in the forward part of the ship could not be taken off due to the fire amidships, so had to slide down ropes into the sea where they were picked up by *HMAS Yarra*'s boats. Many had rope burns on their hands which prevented them from handling weapons during the next week's fighting. Casualties were astonishingly light considering the severity and duration of the attack; three officers had been killed, Colonel Fitt, another officer and ten men had been badly burned by the explosions, and another four men were missing, presumed drowned, after they had jumped over the side during the attack.

Ras Pagani, for whom this was a repeat of his experiences at Dunkirk, nipped below to get his pack in which were photographs of his wife and son. He also brought up his rifle. But all other weapons and equipment went down with the ship and, after they reached Singapore docks in *HMAS Yarra*, Ras had the only shaving kit in his section.

The battalion was re-equipped to a modest scale and put into 18th Division reserve, just north of Bukit Timah village, on 9 February. They were attacked the following day and Ras Pagani realized that the men under his command were not only totally inexperienced in war but had been severely shaken by the bombing at sea and by the general air of defeat on the Island. The next day his platoon was cut off and had to make a wide detour, under fire much of the time, to get back to Battalion HQ in the region of Mount Pleasant. On 15 February their positions were heavily mortared but they held their ground. During the afternoon Ras was ordered to collect all arms and put them in a central point as orders had come that Singapore would capitulate that evening. Colonel Fitt had gone into hospital the previous day for long-overdue treatment for his severe burns and Major D. R. Mullineux had assumed command. Ras Pagani approached him, said that he was unable to comply with the order to surrender and intended to try to escape. Mullineux wished him luck and Ras set off at dusk towards Singapore docks.

As he passed through the deserted streets of Singapore it was like a journey through Hell; fires raged unchecked because there was no water with which to quench them and buildings frequently collapsed with a roar, sending flames and sparks up into the sky. Dead soldiers and civilians lay in the roads and a truck, set on fire by shelling, blazed furiously, the dead occupants still sitting in it like flaming torches. The stench was foul and he was relieved when he arrived at last at the docks. Several motor launches were tied up to the quay but he was unable to start the engines of any of them. Suddenly he spotted a small *sampan* about 15 feet long. It was loaded with fish manure which stank abominably, but it had a rudder and a small square sail, so he decided to take it.

He cast off the painter, pushed the boat away from the dockside and hoisted the sail. Slowly the little boat drew away from the dock as Ras Pagani set forth on his second 'Dunkirk'. Last time he had been with his regiment in a ship crossing the Channel to Dover; now he was alone in a frail *sampan* with over two thousand miles of sailing ahead of him before he could reach the safety of Australia.

It was a daunting prospect but somehow he was confident that he would get there.

CHAPTER ONE

Out of the Fire: Into the Storm

The *sampan* crept slowly across the calm water. The pitch darkness ahead was accentuated by the glare from astern where Singapore lay burning and dying. There was little breeze but, occasionally, when burning buildings collapsed and flames shot upwards, fitful hot gusts ran out across the sea and filled the limp sail.

Slumped at the tiller, Ras Pagani peered into the blackness ahead and struggled to keep awake. Lack of sleep during the fighting of the past few days had completely exhausted him and he realized that, if he was going to keep the boat on course, he would have to get some sleep ashore.

Suddenly a small island loomed out of the darkness to starboard and he quickly turned the *sampan* towards it. As the boat grounded gently on the beach he lowered the sail, jumped over the side and hauled it under cover of some overhanging branches where he made it fast. Thick bushes grew nearby so he wormed his way into them and made himself comfortable. Within minutes he was in a deep sleep, untroubled by the numerous mosquitoes or by thoughts of the holocaust out of which he had escaped.

When he woke the sun was high in the sky and he judged that it was mid-afternoon. His sleep had refreshed him but he was tormented by a raging thirst. He crawled cautiously through the undergrowth and at last found a trickle of water which was enough to slake his thirst. He explored the shore-line and found the wreckage of a small boat named *Shangri La*, but there was no sign of its owners nor was anyone else on the island.

He had no sooner returned to his hide than his eyes were drawn to a nearby island on which were some buildings.* A crowded launch was approaching it. At first he thought that it might be carrying another party of escapers but, when it reached the beach and the occupants jumped ashore, he saw that they were Japanese soldiers carrying rifles with bayonets fixed. They ran up the shore and disappeared among the buildings. He stayed hidden and alert, hoping that they would not investigate his island next. After about an hour they re-embarked and the launch headed north towards the docks.

This close call with the enemy brought home to him that it would be too risky to travel except by night, moving from island to island and lying up each day on one of them. During his schooldays in France he had studied the stars, so navigation at night held no fears for him even though he had no maps, charts or compass. It would be a very long voyage to Australia but his native boat was unlikely to attract much attention and he would just have to take his time. There was an hour or so of daylight left so he lay back and dozed.

* St John's Island, the Quarantine Station.

He was still in sight of Singapore. The inferno of the previous night seemed less horrifying in daylight but fires still raged and on occasions he heard muffled thumps as fuel or ammunition dumps exploded. To the north of Singapore a vast column of black smoke rose high into the sky, as it had done for the past week, covering everything with black oily smuts whenever rain fell.

Compared with the deafening racket of gunfire and bombing over the past days, the present silence seemed almost eerie. It was as if Singapore had at last died and was now at rest.

As soon as darkness fell he set off. The night passed quietly and, just before dawn, he landed on an island occupied by a family of Malays. They were friendly, giving him food and keeping watch while he slept. In the evening he bade them farewell and continued his journey. The food and rest had dispelled all his battle exhaustion and, as the little boat sailed quietly south, he felt confident that his escape would be successful.

Early in the morning he stopped at an island where he found a Chinese *towkay*. The latter was so pleased to see him that, after Ras had fed and slept, he produced some bottles and insisted that Ras join him in a drinking session while they talked. By nightfall Ras, suffering from a very thick head, was thankful to escape from his bibulous host and to continue his voyage.

Before dawn on 19 February he pulled in to another island where, to his astonishment, he found a party of British soldiers. They told him that the island was named Moro and that they were part of the 'escape chain' to Sumatra, which had been organized before the fall of Singapore. Their job was to provision escapers and, when

no more came, to make their way to Sumatra which was
not yet in Japanese hands. They advised Ras to go to
Sumatra as his chances of getting to Australia in such a
small boat would be minimal. After a sleep and some food
he prepared to sail on that evening and decided that he
would not land again before reaching Sumatra. Just as he
was leaving they called him back and gave him a five-
gallon tin full of army rations, including a bottle of rum.

He made fair progress during that night and the
following day although he suffered from cramp because he
was not able to move much in the boat; and the sun beat
down on him and made his stinking cargo of fish manure
even more pungent. Dusk brought him some relief and he
decided to push on in spite of his discomfort.

During the night the wind freshened and the sea rose,
strong gusts buffeting the frail craft. Soon it began to blow
hard and, as the boat was in danger of capsizing, he
hurriedly lowered the sail and secured it. It was not a
moment too soon; the wind rose to a roar and waves broke
against the sides of the boat, drenching him with spray. As
the *sampan* tossed madly about out of control he was afraid
that he would be thrown into the sea. He crawled
amidships and lay flat on his reeking cargo, stretched
across the boat and clinging to the gunwales for dear life.
Waves broke over him continually and, as the fish manure
became sodden, the *sampan* lost some of her buoyancy and
took longer to right herself after each wave had rolled her
on her gunwales. For the first time Ras felt really
frightened; soon she would roll right over for the last time
and he would be drowned – no man could live in that sea
for long. If *only* he had shovelled the fish manure over the
side before the storm she would have been able to recover
more quickly after each wave. But it was too late now; if he

were to relax his hold on the gunwale he would be overboard in no time. For hours – it seemed an eternity – he clung on desperately, soaked, numbed with cold and becoming increasingly exhausted. The wind was now screaming out of the darkness, plucking at him as if to drag him into the sea, and foaming waves broke over the boat so that he was often submerged in the surf which poured over him. The end must be near, he thought miserably; he found a little strength for a prayer but, in his heart, could find no hope of survival.

Then, just before dawn, the gale dropped as suddenly as it had blown up although a very steep sea remained. A faint hope of survival began to creep into his numbed mind but he dared not yet relinquish his hold on the boat until the waves had subsided further.

At first light he could just make out a dark line on the water dead ahead. He prayed that it might be land and not a low bank of cloud. Stiff, soaked and frozen he let go the gunwale and crawled to the sail. With numbed fingers he untied the lashing with difficulty and hoisted the sail. He had no idea where the storm had driven him and his first thought was to get ashore on the first bit of land and empty the *sampan* of the sodden fish manure before sailing on anywhere.

As the sun rose behind him he saw that he was lying about a mile from low-lying land and in the wide mouth of a river* where the sea was becoming calmer. Hurriedly he set course for the river, anxious to get off the open sea in case the wind should suddenly blow up again and take him away from the land. He decided to leave the emptying of the boat until later and push on up the river in the hope

* The Inderagiri River

of finding a village where he could get some food and water.

After creeping up the river for several hours he saw some people on the south bank of the river. As he drew near they waved to him and made signs that he should come ashore. Suddenly he saw that they were British soldiers, so he headed towards the shore and beached the *sampan* near them. He was so stiff, exhausted and bruised that they had to help him from the boat. As he staggered ashore, his uniform soaked and reeking of fish manure, they told him that he was lucky to have survived the storm which had swept that coast during the night.* They were another link in the escape chain and, after giving him a hot drink and some food, they took charge of his *sampan* and put him on a lorry which carried him to Rengat, a small town lying some fifty miles further up the river.

As the lorry ground along the track Ras felt a sense of immense relief, mingled with pride; he was a physical wreck and stank like a midden but he had made it. He was ashore and alive in Sumatra – far more than he had dared to hope for during that terrible night of storm. The first stage of his escape to freedom had, by a miracle, been completed, although he felt that he had died several deaths in achieving it.

---

* This gale is remembered even today by other escapers who were lucky enough to be in more seaworthy craft.

CHAPTER TWO

Captured by the Japanese, and a Journey North

Ras Pagani gratefully abandoned himself to the escape organization which fed him and arranged his onward journey by road and rail to Padang, a port on the west coast of Sumatra. He arrived there on about 1 March and was billeted with other escapers in a large house which stood in its own grounds. There were no restrictions on their movements and they just hung about hopefully waiting for a ship to come and take them to Colombo or Bombay. Some ships had already arrived and had sailed for India, loaded with as many men (including some women and children) as could be crammed into them.* But there were more men in Padang than these ships could carry and Pagani was among those left to hope that further ships would come.

It was not to be; a Dutch ship, *S.S. Palopo*, sailed from Padang early on the morning of 7 March and proved to be the last ship to get out of Padang.

---

* Several were sunk in the Indian Ocean by Japanese submarines, with the loss of virtually all passengers and crews. Pagani owes his life to having failed to get a place on one of these ill-fated ships.

Those remaining waited in vain for rescue. On 15 March they were told that Japanese troops were approaching Padang and that it would be wise to stay off the streets after 10 pm that night.

Ras Pagani could not bear to think that his perilous voyage from Singapore to Sumatra had been in vain so he got together with some survivors of *H.M.S. Prince of Wales.* Moored alongside the dock was a small steam tug which normally operated in the harbour. Being only just over thirty feet long and of a venerable age, it was hardly a suitable candidate for a sixteen-hundred mile sea journey to Colombo, but it was the only vessel available and the situation was now desperate. They loaded it with supplies and prepared it for sea. On 17 March they steamed across the harbour, a few hours ahead of the arrival of the Japanese Army. But, to their astonishment and chagrin, just as they were clearing the harbour, a detachment of Indonesian soldiers fired a machine-gun across their bows and ordered them to put back to the dockside.*

Filled with a sense of frustration and disappointment, Ras watched the Japanese arrive. He had not previously seen Japanese at close range and was not impressed by them, although he guessed that they could be very dangerous if thwarted in any way. After a good deal of shouting, order and counter-order, they herded the prisoners of war into the Dutch barracks. These numbered approximately 1200, including Australians and Dutch, and of this total about 500 were British from various units.

The Japanese were quite unprepared for the task of administering their prisoners so they took the easy way

---

* They would have had little chance, at that late stage, of getting out of the sight of the Japanese and would undoubtedly have been bombed and sunk.

out and left them to look after themselves within the confines of the barracks. No rations were issued; food was supplied by a Chinese contractor and paid for by the prisoners.

As a result of this lack of contact with the Japanese, there was little or no ill-treatment of PoWs at this time. Each nationality set up its own administration but, although life was reasonably easy, everyone suffered from acute boredom. To counter this among the British, Major Apthorp organized classes in trades and education and enlisted Ras Pagani to teach French.

However, after a few weeks, the Japanese realized that they had a very cheap labour force in their care and on 9 May told Apthorp to form a unit of twenty officers and 480 men. These were then split into four companies for administration and taken by rail to Fort de Kok, about one hundred miles north of Padang.

After a night in an empty convent, the party moved in lorries to a school at Kotanopan on 10 May and on to the market town of Taroetoeng the following day. During the journey they passed through jungle, open country and, near Lake Toba, moorland which reminded them of England. On the evening of 12 May they by-passed Medan and arrived at the little port of Belawan Deli. Here they were put in a Dutch internment camp at Uni Kampong where the inmates welcomed them and supplied them with food and clothing.

On 15 May, leaving behind one man who was too sick to travel, they embarked in a ship named *England Maru*. They were battened down in the holds where there was barely room to lie down, far less to move about. The heat was stifling and food, consisting of rice and a thin vegetable stew, was lowered in buckets. There were no washing facilities and barely enough water to drink. Only a few men at a time were allowed up on deck to perform their natural functions and, as there were many dysentery cases among the men, the stench in the holds soon became overpowering. After a day's delay they sailed to join a convoy carrying Australians from Singapore and set course north for southern Burma.

Ras Pagani accepted these discomforts philosophically as the move north was helping his plans for another escape. During the weeks at Padang he had given the matter much thought. He had worked out that there were two major difficulties to be overcome by a European who wished to escape in the Far East. First, the colour, dress and mannerisms of a white man in a native population; second, failure of feet. Any escape would probably entail hundreds of miles of walking: Army boots would be an instant give-away, so it would be necessary to walk barefooted. He had therefore deliberately worn as few clothes as possible and had walked barefooted to harden his feet. By now he was as brown as any native and his feet were hard. The dangers of getting hookworm, which doctors stressed to those who walked barefooted, seemed to him to be a lesser evil than recapture because his feet had failed him during an escape.

After dropping off some Australians at Victoria Point, the convoy arrived at Mergui on 25 May. Here they worked on an extension of the airfield. Living conditions were poor, the work was arduous and, although the Japanese did not bother them much provided the work was done to their satisfaction, there were several instances of severe beatings and other ill-treatment.

The PoWs responded by doing the least work they thought they could get away with and, in defiance of

Japanese orders, supplemented their meagre rations from native sources.

On arrival at Mergui, Ras Pagani had told Major Apthorp that he would not work on a Japanese military installation as a matter of principle (although his real reason was that he wished to conserve his health and strength for his future escape). Apthorp accepted his reason and set him to work in the camp hospital which was rapidly filling due to disease and overwork on an inadequate diet. But to some officers, who had the unenviable task of organizing the outside work and protecting their men by keeping the Japanese reasonably happy, Ras was a thorn in their flesh. (None of them had any idea of his real purpose in being uncooperative.)

On 11 August they re-embarked in two small ships and sailed for a day to Tavoy where, again, they worked on the airfield and also in the town. Due to the excesses of the pro-Japanese Burma Independent Army (BIA), in particular against Indians and Karens, a resentment against the Japanese was already growing among the civilian population. PoWs working in the town were surreptitiously slipped gifts of food, money and medicines and, eventually, parts for a wireless receiving set. This was then constructed by Sergeant L. W. Bullock, R.A.F., providing them with their first authentic news from the outside world since their capture. (Bullock continued to operate the set until 1944 and, with similar sets in other camps, PoWs were well-informed and their morale benefited enormously).

Ras Pagani, perhaps unwisely in view of the advantages to be gained from the 'town working parties', again refused to leave camp and continued his work in the hospital.

The death and sickness rate of PoWs, which had been so high in Mergui, had decreased with the better conditions in Tavoy but, inevitably, there was a gradual decline in the health of all prisoners with each month spent in captivity.

On 21 October they were again herded into barges and towed down the river to two ships which took them the short journey to Moulmein. They were marched to the gaol, a rewarding progress because, in spite of all efforts by the Japanese to keep them away, the local people crowded round and showered the PoWs with food and fruit until the Japanese guards began to lose their tempers at this obvious display of sympathy for the prisoners.

The following day they journeyed by train about thirty miles to Thanbyuzayat, a station on the railway which ran south from Moulmein to Ye, and the intended junction of the railway to Bangkok which they were now to build.

The railway trace had already been cut and camps had been established about every five kilometres along the line, some being occupied by PoWs and others by Burmese labourers. Japanese Army railway construction units directed the work but took no interest in the prisoners apart from extracting from them as much work as possible. Camps were administered by a staff commanded by Colonel Nagitomo, but, as usual, the Japanese were very inefficient in organizing the camps and this duty was virtually taken over by Brigadier Varley, the senior Australian officer, who, with a small staff, ran the camps from Thanbyuzayat. As Nagitomo was helpless without Brigadier Varley's team, the prisoners were on a good wicket and lack of co-operation was usually enough to bring Nagitomo to heel. Consequently, the subsequent death rate on the railway in Burma was about ten per cent, whereas in Siam, where the Japanese assumed full control of the work force, it was over thirty per cent.

After a delay of a few days in Thanbyuzayat the British (Sumatra) PoW Battalion – now reduced by death and sickness to about 400 officers and men from the original 500 who had left Padang in March, – marched to a hutted camp at Hlepauk, 18 Km up the railway trace. Built in a valley and adjacent to the road and a small stream, the camp consisted of a clearing in an area covered with clumps of bamboo and scrub jungle. Nearby a range of jungle-covered hills rose to about a thousand feet.

During the march Ras Pagani studied the countryside as he was determined to escape at the first opportunity. The day after their arrival Colonel Nagitomo came to the camp and made a speech to the inmates. It contained the usual mixture of friendliness and threats and was couched in hysterically funny English in the original. The result, when it reached the ears of the prisoners, after a grammatical mangling by the Japanese interpreter, rendered it quite incomprehensible. Nagitomo emphasized the impossibility of successful escape as follows:—

'You should therefore be contented accordingly. If there is a man here who has at least one per cent of a chance of escape we shall make him face the extreme penalty. If there is one foolish man who is trying to escape, he shall see big jungles toward the east which are absolutely impossible for communication, towards the west he shall see the boundless ocean, and above all, in the main points of south and north our Nippon Army is staying and guarding. You will easily understand the difficulties of complete escape. A few such cases of ill-omened matters which happened in Singapore* shall

* A reference to the execution, by a firing party of Sikhs under Japanese supervision, of Corporal Breavington and Private V. L. Gale of the A.I.F., and two others after recapture following their attempted escape.

prove the above and you should not repeat such foolish things although it is a last chance after great embarrassment.'*

It was now the end of October, 1942, and work on the railway was accelerating. The Japanese allowed only sick men to remain in camp and Ras Pagani now had to go to work on the line. The work was hard and the Japanese engineers, in their customary manner, having set a 'norm', and seen that PoWs were achieving it, then increased it. Tasks then became impossible to complete except by working for longer hours. As the sickness rate began to rise the fit men were driven even harder by the Japanese until everyone was exhausted and virtually sick. In the camp living conditions were bad; huts leaked so that men were always soaked and few had spare clothes or any bedding. The frequent rains turned the working area into a knee-deep sea of mud.

Ras Pagani realized that he would probably be living under those conditions for months, perhaps even years. Each month that passed would further undermine his health until he would reach a point where he would be physically incapable of making an arduous escape. It was now or never; he began to put together his ideas for a breakout.

He had formed two plans. The first was to go to the sea – about ten miles away – steal a boat and make his way along the coast to Upper Burma. If he was unable to find a boat he would double back to the Ye-Moulmein railway and follow it north to Moulmein and beyond. Moulmein would be a very dangerous place for him. It was heavily populated, teemed with Japanese troops and their allies,

* *Three Times a Guest, Recollections of Japan and the Japanese 1942–1969.* Charles A. Fisher, Cassell, London, 1979.

the pro-Japanese BIA, and every bridge and ferry across the Salween River would undoubtedly be closely watched, especially as the Japanese would guess, correctly, that he had no option but to travel north.

But the obstacles to the success of this second plan were formidable and would have deterred all but the most determined from attempting such an escape. Our nearest forces – in the Arakan – were over six hundred miles north as the crow flew and he would probably have to cover at least a thousand miles on foot. He knew nothing of the various races who lived in Burma, had no idea whether they would be helpful or hostile to him, and, apart from a rough and ready Hindustani which he had picked up during his two years service in India, he spoke no language other than French and English. In his low state of health he would be vulnerable to diseases such as malaria and dysentery and, apart from having no medicines, would have no one to care for him should he fall ill. In addition there would be a price of Rs250 on his head.

On the credit side, he was now as brown as a native, his feet were hard, his Italian forbears had bequeathed him dark brown eyes – another essential if impersonating any Eastern race – his height of 5′ 5″ was about right and hard work, combined with poor diet, had slimmed him down. He also sported a formidable auburn beard. Finally, the Japanese would be looking for an escaped Englishman, whereas he intended to dress, act and walk like an Indian.

He had made up his mind to go and was confident that, if the preparation and thought which he had put into his plan was helped by some luck, he would get away with it.

He had spoken to no one in the camp about his plans, partly for the need for security, partly because he did not

want to involve anyone else with a knowledge of his escape
in case the Japanese threatened reprisals on his mates, but
mainly because, as the risks were so great, he felt that he
could not ask anyone else to share them. Nor did he wish
to be responsible for a companion during such an arduous
and risky enterprise.

It was now about 12 November and he decided to select
a suitable moment to leave camp. He would abandon his
meagre possessions and clothing as these would mark him
as an escaped PoW. He would carry a little money and
wear only a loincloth and *pāgri*. For the time being he
would hold on to his identity discs so that he could prove
his identity to our own forces and also prove to the
Japanese, if he were to be recaptured, that he was a British
soldier and not a native spy. These he would hide inside
his *pāgri*.

Two days later his plans were completed. The day for
which he had so long prepared himself had arrived and he
knew that, even if he lived to an old age, this decision was
probably the most important that he would make in his
lifetime.

At dawn he had breakfast, attended *tenko* and then
joined the men who were reporting sick. The Japanese
always attended the sick parade and any man whom they
judged to be malingering was beaten up for wasting good
working time, awarded a kick up the arse to the accom-
paniment of much shouted abuse, given a *changkul* and
told to join the working party at once. So confident were
they that escape was impossible they never sent a guard
with those whom they drove out to join the working party.

Ras Pagani took his beating and abuse and left camp
alone carrying his *changkul* which he resolved to keep as a
weapon.

When he was a hundred yards from the camp gate he looked round to make sure that no Japanese were watching him and slipped quickly into the jungle.

A wave of elation came over him; he was starting his long haul to freedom.

CHAPTER THREE

Escape from the Railway of Death and a Meeting with Friends

He set off in a westerly direction. At first he made good progress but at times he came up against very thick jungle which slowed him down.

Time was absolutely vital to the success of his escape. He had planned to give himself a clear twenty-four hours in which to put as much distance as possible between him and the camp. He knew he would not be missed until the evening *tenko* and guessed that the Japanese would not search for him during the hours of darkness. But, if his first plan failed, he would have to come back part of the way in order to pick up the railway and put his second plan into operation so it was essential that he should continue his journey during the first night in order to get well away from the camp.

The ten-mile journey to the sea took him four hours. By bad luck he hit a part of the coast where there were no villages and, therefore, no boats. He could not afford the time to search the coastline for a boat so promptly started on his second plan. He headed off in a north-easterly direction, reached the railway in the afternoon and

followed it north to Thanbyuzayat, the outskirts of which
he approached late in the afternoon. He knew Thanbyuzayat was only 18 km from the camp; he dared not waste
time waiting for darkness so he wound on his *pāgri*, rubbed
dirt on his face, arms and legs, and walked boldly down
the main street of the village. This was broad, with wide
verges, and he walked as fast as he could and in the
manner in which he had seen Indians walk. But his
disguise was not as good as he had hoped. He noticed
several villagers staring at him and heard them muttering
among themselves but the only word he could understand
was '*Nippon*'* However, they made no attempt to detain
him and he pushed on hoping that no one would challenge
him.

Suddenly, to his horror, he saw a Japanese guard of five
soldiers, commanded by a sergeant, coming line-abreast
up the street towards him. For a split second he was
overwhelmed by fear and his instinct was to run. If the
villagers had easily penetrated his disguise as an Indian so
too might the Japanese and that would be the end of his
escape and probably his life.

But his self-control took over and he forced himself to
walk towards them for a few more yards. Then, almost
casually, he strolled over to a gateway which led to a house
and squatted down, Indian fashion, to pee, keeping his
back towards the approaching Japanese.

His heart thumped and he was so tensed up that he was
unable to pass any water but continued to squat and held
his breath as the sound of Japanese boots grew louder.

Every moment he expected to hear them shout

---

* He heard later that the Japanese often disguised themselves as natives
and moved among the local population to spy on them. Often they pounced
on a villager whom they suspected and hung him from a tree.

'*Kurrah!*'* and run over to capture him. But, after one of the longest minutes of his life, they passed him and continued up the street. Ras heaved a sigh of relief; it had been a narrow squeak and he saw that, in his anxiety to get far away from the camp, he had made a mistake in trying to pass through the village in daylight.

When he considered it was safe he rose, rejoined the road and continued his journey, but now he was looking desperately for a place in which he could hide until dark. The chance came soon; he entered the market place, which was not operating at that time of day, and spotted a stall near a wall. The stall had a curtain round its base which would conceal him. After looking about carefully to see if anyone was watching him, he crawled behind the curtain. He still had his *changkul* and, although it was not much of a weapon, it gave him confidence; its use might just gain him that vital second or two in which to break away if he was detected.

There were only about two hours of daylight left and, as he was tired by his journey of some twenty miles, he fell into a light sleep almost at once.

When he woke it was dark. He crawled out of his hiding place and set off again down the street until he reached the railway line which ran north to Moulmein.

It dawned on him that he would travel much faster, and it would be less hard on his bare feet, if he were to walk on the railway sleepers. His lack of height and short legs made each pace rather a long stretch but he soon got into the right rhythm and covered much more ground than he would have done if finding his way across country in the dark.

* Stop!/Come here!

His meeting with the Japanese in Thanbyuzayat had shaken him and he resolved, as on his escape by sea from Singapore, to lie hidden each day sleeping, and, if possible, getting some food. At first light he could see that the railway was running across *padi* fields and, out in one of these fields, well away from the line, was an isolated native hut. He made his way to it and found it was the home of an Indian family. Using signs and his Hindustani he made them understand that he wanted to stay for the day and sleep. They chattered among themselves and then the husband said, '*Thik hai*'* and beckoned him into the hut. They fed him on rice, *dāl* and tea, and gave him a place to sleep, making him understand that they would keep an eye out for any Japanese.

They woke him late in the afternoon and gave him another meal. After he had thanked them, one of the children guided him round a small village and back onto the railway line. Ras thanked the child who gave him a smiling farewell before returning to his house.

There was a bright moon and he moved fast along the sleepers. After his fright of the previous day his confidence had returned and he had been very cheered by the friendly sanctuary given him by the Indians. He decided to hide with Indians throughout the next day if possible.

There were two major obstacles two or three days' journey ahead: Moulmein, through or round which he would have to travel, and the crossing of the Salween River. Both these would prove a severe test and he would need much luck.

Soon after midnight he saw the lights of a town ahead of him. This puzzled him; he had no map but had a rough

* OK.

idea of the distance from Thanbyuzayat to Moulmein and he estimated he was covering about twelve miles each night. Surely this town could not be Moulmein which he had not expected to reach for another two or three nights?* The railway line would lead to a station in the town and he was determined not to enter a town again even by night. When he was about a mile from the outskirts he left the line and made a wide detour. The sky had now clouded over so that he could not see the stars and he began to lose his direction as he plunged through the *padi* and patches of thorny scrub. He kept the lights of the town in sight to his right side but, even when he had passed the town, he could not find the railway again. He began to get worried; in a few hours it would be light and he was still far too close to the town for safety.

Then, suddenly, he was back on the line and he followed it north as fast as he could in order to get well away from the town.

At dawn he again chose an isolated hut in the *padi*, and, again, it was the home of an Indian family. They were surprised and seemed rather nervous when he appeared but, at last, invited him in. After he had fed they gave him a place in which to sleep but, for some reason, he was uneasy and slept only fitfully. These Indians seemed more on edge than those of the previous day and he wondered whether the Japanese had already posted a reward for his capture in Moulmein and the surrounding villages, and whether these Indians had heard of it and were debating if they should betray him and claim the reward.

However, his fears proved groundless. After a meal in the evening, they sent him on his way. But the risks

---

* It was Mudon, about 24 km south of Moulmein.

entailed by contact with local people was beginning to play on his nerves, especially now that he was approaching Moulmein. His fears were allayed to some extent by the friendliness of the Indians who he had so far met and he really had no alternative but to accept the risk if he was to get food and sleep during the hours of daylight. Nevertheless, the dangers nagged at his mind.

He walked on all night meeting no one. By dawn he was within a few miles of Moulmein. He left the railway and approached a hut. An Indian came out and, after a short conversation, Ras saw that he had had a real stroke of fortune in choosing this hideout. The man, who introduced himself as Mohammed Esoof, said that he had served for several years in the Indian Army and was very pro-British. He said that he would help Ras on his journey but added that it would be far too dangerous to enter Moulmein or try to cross the Salween there as the town was full of Japanese, BIA and their informers. By good fortune he had a brother who was a fisherman and lived on the island of Bilugyun which lay in the mouth of the Salween River. Ras must wait for a day while Mohammed Esoof's son went to the island and fetched his uncle.

Ras relaxed. He felt no fear here as he trusted Mohammed Esoof implicitly. The family fed him well and he sat talking to his host about India and the Army.

The next day the son returned accompanied by his uncle. The latter agreed to take Ras to his home on the island that night and, the following night, to take him on to the north bank. Thus he would bypass Moulmein and Martaban to the west.

Ras heaved a sigh of relief. The dangers of having to get through Moulmein and across the Salween had been preying on his mind for days and now the problem had been solved for him at a stroke. If he continued to have luck like this nothing could prevent his escape.

They travelled together that night, crossed by boat to the island and by dawn Ras had been fed and was fast asleep in the fisherman's hut.

Before leaving that night he wrote out a chit saying that the fisherman had helped him to escape and presented it to him. The man was delighted and, after they had eaten and darkness had fallen, they got into the boat and headed north across the estuary of the Salween. The journey took about an hour. Ras could see the lights of Moulmein and Martaban due east of him two or three miles away and was thankful that he was not trying to get through these towns.

The boat grounded gently on the north shore. Ras, still clutching his *changkul*, jumped ashore and whispered his thanks to the fisherman who then pushed off into the night.

When he had got his bearings he set off in a northerly direction and before long had picked up the railway which was now running in a west-nor-west direction. Determined to get as far from Moulmein as possible during the night he pushed on at his fastest speed. When dawn came he found that he had left the *padi* and had entered heavily forested country. There was no sign of any Indian hut so he left the railway and made a hide in a thicket. He realized he would have to go without food for the day but he had been well fed by his last hosts so this was no great hardship. He slept all day and at dusk came back to the railway and followed it north.

At dawn he saw that the woods had become more orderly, like plantations rather than jungle. He left the railway and moved on cautiously through the trees until he saw some buildings ahead of him. He crept forward to within a hundred yards of them and lay and watched them for hours. He saw that the people who lived in the house were not Burmese; they had fair skin and the women's clothes were red and white. There was an air of prosperity about the place and, as he guessed that people who had been prosperous under the British were unlikely to look with much favour on the Japanese, he decided to approach them for help.

The front entrance was just off a small road and he felt that, if the people were hostile and tried to arrest him, the scuffle would be seen by other people who lived nearby and might help to catch him. As he was dressed as an Indian worker and in a fairly dirty state, it would be more appropriate to go to the back door from which he had seen servants coming and going all day about their business. If any effort was made to catch him he would have a chance of darting back into the trees and getting well away before anyone could mobilize a search party.

Grasping his *changkul*, he walked quickly to the back door and knocked on it. It was opened by a surprised servant girl. Ras made signs and spoke a few words of Hindustani; motioning to him to wait, she went back into the house.

Ras waited anxiously, gripping his *changkul* and glancing nervously around him, ready to defend himself and dash back into the trees if anyone tried to detain him. After what seemed an hour but was only a few minutes, the door opened again and in front of him stood a well-dressed and very beautiful girl. She looked him up and down for a moment and, before he could open his mouth to speak, said, in perfect English, 'Please come in'.

He was so flabbergasted that he stood rooted to the

ground, totally at a loss for words. She smiled at him, then reached out and gently took his *changkul* which she handed to the goggle-eyed servant girl behind her. Again she asked him to come in.

Pulling himself together at last, Ras muttered, 'Thank you very much,' and followed her into the house. She led him to a comfortable sitting room where she asked him to sit down for a moment while she went to send a servant to tell her father of her unusual guest. When she had gone it suddenly struck Ras forcibly that she had known at once that he was English even though he had said no word. His disguise, which he had thought so convincing, she had seen through in an instant.

Still absolutely bewildered by this turn of events, he lowered himself into an arm-chair and looked round the room. It was furnished just like a Victorian drawing room in England – lace curtains, Victorian furniture and several small tables on which were framed portraits. The only thing which contradicted the illusion that he was at home was the electric fan hanging from the ceiling.

The incongruity of the situation struck him forcibly; a few minutes earlier he had been, to all intents and purposes, an Indian labourer, none too clean from living rough, and on the run. Suddenly, he was sitting here in this elegant room, within a stone's throw of the jungle, still a work-begrimed Indian and the guest of a lovely girl who spoke English as well as he did.

This transformation of his circumstances was like a dream and he could hardly believe that it was real. It was as if God had directed his footsteps to this haven of safety.

CHAPTER FOUR

Journey to the Karen Hills

After a short while the girl returned and said that her father would return home that evening. She chatted to Ras about her family who were Karen Christians and told him that her father's name was Saw Po Thin. He was a very influential timber merchant who had been contracted by the Japanese to produce sleepers for the railway which they were building to Siam. Because he was of use to them the Japanese left him alone and this gave him the opportunity, as Ras was later to discover, of tipping off the Karenni States about Japanese intentions and troop movements against Karen resistance fighters.

His daughter was obviously very sure of their safety from the Japanese and their informers, and sat talking with great composure to Ras, quite unperturbed by her dirty and half-naked guest. She told Ras that the name of this hamlet was Kyawaing and that it was a few miles south of Thaton.

A servant brought in a tea tray and set it on a table. Ras stared with disbelief at the bone china tea set, the thin sandwiches and the English biscuits. He had to keep an iron grip on his manners because he had eaten nothing for forty-eight hours and was as hungry as a horse.

There were further surprises in store for him. After tea she showed him to a bedroom in which was a four-poster bed fitted with a mosquito net. On the bed was a clean set of Karen clothes for him. There was a bathroom next door and he spent an hour scrubbing himself until the water was black.

All this luxury confirmed his guess that Saw Po Thin was a very wealthy man and he blessed the good fortune which had brought him to this house.

It was 7 pm by the time Ras came back into the drawing room, clean and arrayed in his Karen outfit. Meanwhile his host had returned and heard from his daughter the story of Ras's arrival. He greeted Ras warmly and later they sat down to an English dinner in his honour, roast peacock taking the place of turkey or chicken. After the meal they sat and talked far into the night. In spite of his journey the previous night and lack of sleep during the day, Ras was so elated that he felt no fatigue. He regaled Saw Po Thin with the story of his escape from Singapore, his life as a PoW and his journey from 18 Km camp. He learned that Saw Po Thin and all his family had been educated in England and had a great admiration for the English. He said that Ras must stay with him for a few days while arrangements were made for him to continue his journey north.

Ras then confided to his host his intention to get to our forces in northern Burma, to tell them what was happening to PoWs on the railway and to continue the fight against the Japanese in Burma. He asked Saw Po Thin to help him achieve this aim.

The latter considered this proposal in silence for a

minute. It would, he said, be difficult – perhaps impossible – to move an Englishman west to the Bassein area,
where there were many Karens, without him being
detected and betrayed by the Burmese who were pre-
dominant in the open country north of Rangoon. He
would be in constant danger and so would be his Karen
guides. However, once in Bassein, the Karens there, who
were constantly harassed by the BIA and carefully
watched by the Japanese and their spies, would undoubtedly help him. It might not be too difficult to pass him
north, over the Irrawaddy River and into the Arakan
Yomas where the hills were heavily forested and the
Karens living there would befriend him and guide him
north. Saw Po Thin said that he knew nothing of the
situation in the north of the country but was doubtful if
guides could be found who would dare to try and take him
through the battle zone where concentrations of Japanese
would be heavy and the wild country was a hotbed of
malaria and other tropical diseases.

Seeing the growing disappointment on Ras's face, Saw
Po Thin put to him an alternative plan. There was, he
said, a British major who, instead of withdrawing to India
with the rest of the Burma army, had elected to remain in
the Karen hills in order to raise and train Karen guerrillas
to fight the Japanese. He was in hiding only a few days'
journey away. Would Ras like to be taken to him and then,
perhaps, to continue his journey north from there? If he
would like this it could easily be arranged in a few days.
(He did not divulge to Ras that he had already sent a
runner to the major, reporting Ras's arrival and asking if
he should be sent on.)

Ras thought hard for several minutes about these two
options. His object in escaping had been to get back into

the war. His recent luck led him to believe that, with the help of Saw Po Thin and other Karens, he would probably achieve his aim of reaching our forces in the Arakan.

Nevertheless, the prospect of joining a British officer who was running the resistance in the Karenni States held great appeal for him and would, he felt, put the final seal of success on his escape.*

While Ras turned these matters over in his mind, his host sat silent, watching him. At last, his mind made up, Ras agreed to go to the British officer. Saw Po Thin appeared very relieved at this decision and said that he would arrange the move as soon as possible. Meanwhile Ras must rest and eat well because the journey would be arduous and dangerous.

After two days the runner returned with a message from the major who said that Ras should be sent to him, but added, ominously, that if he had been infiltrated by the Japanese in the guise of an escaped prisoner of war, then he would be executed in the Karenni States.†

After reading the message Saw Po Thin sought out Ras and told him that he would be leaving for the Karen hills the following day, and hurried off to make the necessary arrangements for the journey.

Ras was woken in the early hours of the following morning and given a meal. Then he was taken outside to a bullock cart and told to lie down on the floor. A box, like an upturned coffin, was put over him and the cart was then loaded very high with stinking rubbish of all kinds.

* Today he is confident that he would have reached the Arakan with the help of the Karens but he also feels that it was God's will that he should have chosen to go to help Seagrim whom he regards as no less than a saint, as do the Karens.

† Such an infiltraton actually occurred in Malaya. See *A Fearful Freedom* by the author, Leo Cooper, 1984.

Luckily the planks of the cart floor were separated by gaps so that he was able to breathe freely but, nevertheless, the stench was ghastly and he wished he had had a gas mask. However, the safety value of the reeking load became apparent after only half an hour's journey when the cart stopped at a Japanese check point in Thaton. Ras could hear the Japanese joking among themselves about the stink and urging the driver to get away quickly.

Although they met no more Japanese Ras was forced to stay under his odoriferous covering all day.

At dusk the cart stopped, the driver jettisoned his load and helped Ras to get out from under the box. He asked Ras if he could swim and, when Ras confirmed that he could, they left the bullock cart and walked in the dark for about three miles to a small cluster of huts where he was given water, a meal and a place to sleep.

In the morning they set off again and, after covering a few miles, came to a deep and fast-flowing river about twenty-five yards wide. They swam across and entered bamboo and scrub jungle. After about three miles they came out on to a dirt road where a bullock cart was waiting for them. Ras was most impressed by the arrangements which Saw Po Thin had made for his journey. His escort introduced Ras to the driver of the bullock cart, Saw Willie Saw, who had worked as a forest ranger for the British, and bade him farewell as he retraced his steps to Thaton.

Ras got into the cart and they set off. He was amazed by the change in his mode of life. Here there was no question of hiding; they rode in the cart in broad daylight and exchanged friendly greetings with local people, all of whom seemed happy and relaxed. Ras later found that he was now in the Karenni States where neither the Japanese nor the BIA came, due to their fear of the guerrillas operating under the command of the British Major. Ras suddenly remembered his *changkul* which he had left with Saw Po Thin, but knew that he no longer had any need of it as a weapon.

Before dark they arrived at Saw Willie's Saw's house in the village of Molopa where Ras was introduced to his family and friends. That night the Karens gave a party for him – first, the meal, which consisted of roast pork and peacock, rice and a sweetmeat, and then a drinking session on toddy. Saw Willie Saw told Ras that he must not refuse to take part in the drinking, the aim of which was to see who would be the last man to become insensible. All the men sat round in a circle with the headman in the centre. He was given the first cup and this he gave to the 'Gods' (even though the Karens were Christians they retained some of their pagan rites in their everyday life – perhaps as a form of insurance against the displeasure of their erstwhile pagan gods). The headman emptied the first cup onto the ground on his right side. The cup was refilled and he drank it dry; it was refilled and he took it and passed it to the nearest man on his right who tipped a drop on the ground and then emptied the cup at one gulp. This procedure continued until the cup had passed to every man in the circle. Then the headman drank his second cup and the process started all over again and continued throughout the night.

Ras was uncertain at what stage he passed out but at midday he woke, fully dressed and with a splitting headache. In the doorway of his hut squatted a crowd of grinning Karens. He smiled at them, feeling no resentment at their intrusion because he saw that there was no malice in their amusement; they were just like innocent children in their delight at his plight.

He staggered out into the sunlight and walked over to Saw Willie Saw who told the women to bring Ras some food. After he had eaten this he felt as good as new. Saw Willie Saw advised him to stay there for two days because Ras had a painful cut in one instep which a Karen girl, who had some experience of nursing, dressed for him.

For the next two days he sat around the hamlet talking to the Karens and watching them go about their normal lives. He studied the huts which were built of bamboo and were on stilts. The whole living area was on a platform; in the centre of the platform was a fireplace laid on bricks where the cooking was done, a hole in the roof letting out the smoke. At one end of the platform was the lavatory – a hole cut in the platform over which one squatted. Ras was astounded and then amused the first time he used it, by the squealing and stampeding of the pigs which wandered loose around the huts. He saw that every time anyone went to this lavatory, the pigs all rushed underneath and waited for manna to drop from heaven, squabbling over the results. He could almost measure the disappointment on their faces when they received nothing more than a stream of urine. But the system served to keep the village spotlessly clean, unlike so many of the villages in India which he remembered.

Two days later Saw Willie Saw told him that they were going to 'the priest's house'. An elephant was brought to the door of the hut and Ras was told to get on its neck. He was shown how to guide it; jiggling the toes of his right foot in the elephant's right ear would make it turn to the left and vice versa. If he wanted it to go faster he worked his toes in both ears at the same time. He was accompanied by another elephant with its *oozie*, and one armed guard.

They travelled along a dirt road all the morning, Ras

feeling like a Maharaja. Every time they passed Karens these waved and smiled at him.

At noon they stopped at a village which Ras learned was named Kadaingti (and which was to be his head-quarters in later weeks). The villagers were a mixed lot – Karens, Indians and Gurkhas, the latter having been cut off from their regiment during the fighting at the Sittang bridge – but, of course, no Burmans, because many of these were pro-Japanese and, in any case, did not get on with the Karens, especially after the BIA had persecuted and massacred many Karens in the Delta. They spent the rest of the day and that night at Kadaingti because the elephants did not like travelling after midday in the worst of the heat and also because they had to be fed and watered, a time-consuming process with animals of such large appetites.

They sat about talking, eating and drinking – in moderation on this occasion. It was here that Ras met Lance Naik Mura, an ex-Burma Rifles soldier, whose home was in Assam. He now attached himself to Ras as bodyguard and was to remain with him during the rest of his journey north. The villagers gave Ras a hut to himself for the night and Mura slept across the doorway.

In the morning they continued their journey along the dirt road until noon when they stopped at a village in the jungle. Although the road was still wide and level, the surrounding country was now all jungle and beginning to close in on them.

The following day at noon they arrived at Papun. Ras was taken first to the village shop and then on to an impressive house on a small hill. Here he was introduced to Father Loizeau, an elderly French priest, and it was now that Ras's knowledge of French proved of great advantage because Father Loizeau spoke little English.

They talked together in French for hours, Ras telling the priest of his experiences since he had landed in Singapore. Late at night Father Loizeau showed him to a room and Mura bedded down outside the door.

In the morning the priest asked him if he would like to attend Mass with the villagers. Ras accepted with enthusiasm although he still found the situation incredible as he, a British escaped PoW, knelt with a congregation of Karens in the jungle to celebrate Mass. There was no fear of Japanese or Burmese intervening and so the whole atmosphere was relaxed and friendly.

After Mass Father Loizeau showed him around his grounds. He grew coffee on quite a large scale and all his own vegetables.

At night they had a splendid meal of roast peacock, sweet potatoes and other green vegetables which were unfamiliar to Ras, and Father Loizeau produced a bottle of French red wine. Again they talked late into the night before retiring to bed, Mura sticking like a leech to Ras, although for what purpose the latter could not guess.*

At dawn Mura woke him and Father Loizeau asked if he would like to attend Communion. This Ras refused; he felt that he was on such intimate terms with the good Father that he could not bring himself to make confession to him. Father Loizeau quite understood and gave him his blessing.

Late the following day another French priest arrived whom Father Loizeau introduced in French as Father Calmon, and who was much younger than his superior. After a lengthy conversation the two priests decided to

---

* It is probable that Mura was aware that Ras might one day travel north to join our forces and that he would thus be able to reach his home in Assam.

send a runner to Major Seagrim – the first time Ras had heard the name of 'the British officer in the hills' – to tell him of Ras's arrival in Papun and to ask whether Seagrim would like Ras to come on and meet him.

After about five days the reply came and preparations were made for the journey north. In the morning they set off, a party of eight men led by one Naik Ah Din, and two elephants, on one of which Ras rode. He thought that they would have made quicker progress on foot but supposed that the Karens thought the jungle too dense for an Englishman to get through on foot. As it was, Ras was in great danger of being hit in the face by branches or cut by bamboo. By now they were travelling in very dense jungle and going up and down steep jungle-clad hills. Ras marvelled at the sure-footedness of the elephants; when going uphill they never put a front foot firmly down until they had tested the firmness of the ground with the other front foot. On the downhill slopes they tested the ground first in the same way and then slid down almost on their tails. But this practice made progress very slow.

They travelled in this manner for four days. On the fifth day they left the elephants and went on on foot, making use of streams and thick bamboo jungle in order to leave no tracks.

At last they arrived at a rough bamboo shelter in the jungle; it was occupied by a Kachin who led them on for another fifteen minutes until they reached another jungle hut. Standing on the platform was a tall dark-skinned man, his hair bobbed like a Pathan, dressed in native clothes. Ras assumed he was another native until he jumped down and said, 'Hello old chap. How are you?' as if he was welcoming him to a country house in England. Ras was astounded but, knowing he was a Major, replied,

'O.K. Sir'. The situation was so fantastic that his military training almost made him stand to attention as he addressed the Major, but he just managed to avoid that.

It was a heart-warming meeting. The major, who introduced himself as Hugh Seagrim, grasped Ras's hand and almost shook his arm off as he kept on saying, in a voice filled with emotion, how glad he was that Ras had come. Ras felt tears in his eyes and could hardly speak.

Seagrim talked to the guides and then sent them away except for the faithful Mura. Meanwhile Ras studied the man who was to have such a profound influence on his life; no question here of the usual relationship between a major and a corporal – Ras got the impression that Seagrim had sized him up in an instant and that now they were already firm friends. Ras has always been convinced that God had sent him to Seagrim.

CHAPTER FIVE

Major Seagrim and the Karen Levies

Throughout most of that first night the two men sat and talked. Ras told Seagrim how he had escaped from Singapore and from 18 Km camp. They worked out that during the latter escape he had covered between two hundred and two hundred and fifty miles, most of it walking barefooted, but also using boats, bullock carts and elephants. Including days spent waiting at various stages of the journey, exactly one month had passed since Ras had walked out of the camp.

He put to Seagrim a matter which had been worrying him throughout his journey. The Japanese in 18 Km camp knew him by name and had almost certainly notified other Japanese units and Burmese police stations of his escape. He probably had a price on his head and was well aware that, if recaptured, he would be returned to the camp and shot. Therefore he had not disclosed his surname to any of his helpers, not even to Saw Po Thin and the French missionaries, in the hope of throwing the Japanese off his scent and leading them to assume that, as he had not been sighted, he had probably died of starvation or disease in the jungle not far from the camp. He feared that if the Karens knew his name and gossiped about him in the villages, an informer might tell the Japanese that he had reached the Karenni States.

Seagrim agreed and added that there was also a danger that the Japanese might pick up a Karen for interrogation and, if the man knew Pagani's name, he might divulge it under torture. They decided that he would be known to the Karens only as 'Corporal Ras', a name which the Japanese would not associate with an escaped PoW named Pagani. He felt relieved and much safer now that this matter had been settled.

Seagrim was very impressed, not only by Pagani's successful escape to the Karenni States, but also because Ras had, before leaving camp, worked out that his only chance of success was to travel barefooted, as an Indian, with no betraying 'aids or comforts' to help him on his journey.

During his exploration of the Karen Hills, before the war began, Seagrim had also travelled lighter than most Europeans would have found acceptable and now was dressed like a Karen and lived as one of them. He saw in Ras Pagani an ideal recruit for his operations and a man whom he could trust to get on well with the Karens.

At last, exhausted by talking, they curled up either side of the fire and slept for a few hours.

Ras spent about ten days with Seagrim. During that time he came to admire Seagrim immensely and learned much of his background and his aims for the Karen resistance movement. They very soon became firm friends; Seagrim called Ras by his Christian name and Ras, with the Regular soldier's acknowledgement of rank, at first called Seagrim 'major', then 'skipper' and finally 'skip'. He saw that Seagrim had gone through a period of great loneliness and frustration and that his arrival had stimulated Seagrim and given him back his enthusiasm for welding the Karens into a resistance force.

But, however close was their friendship, Ras became aware, as the days passed, that he was serving under a most remarkable man who had such a love for the Karen people that he was quite prepared to sacrifice his life for them. It was no wonder that Hugh Seagrim came to be regarded by the Karens as their 'father' and, by both Ras Pagani and the Karens, as a saint.

Hugh Paul Seagrim was the youngest of the five sons of the Reverend Charles Seagrim and his wife Amabel. From 1909, until his death in 1927, Charles Seagrim was rector of Whissonsett-with-Horningtoft, two small adjoining villages which lay roughly in the centre of the northern half of Norfolk. Although an able and gifted man, the rector never sought preferment because he was happier to see his five sons growing up in the pleasant atmosphere of the Norfolk countryside.

The Rectory was the hub of these two communities and the boys took part in everything that went on, shooting, riding, and playing in local cricket and football teams. They knew everyone by name in the two villages and there can be little doubt that Hugh's religious background, and the free and easy association with the local people, did much to prepare him for his years of war among the Karen Christians. His strong religious beliefs not only ensured the respect of the Karens and gave him courage and comfort in his dangerous and primitive life in the jungle, but also enabled him to love the Karens in the way that he had loved the villagers of Norfolk, and to receive their genuine love in return.

The Karens called the Japanese 'short legs' and the English 'long legs'. Seagrim was exceptionally tall and was known to them as 'Grandfather Longlegs'.*

It had been intended that Hugh should try for the Royal Navy but, after it had been discovered that he was partially colour-blind, he was debarred from a Naval career, so followed his four elder brothers into the Army. After passing through Sandhurst he was selected for the Indian Army and spent a year in India attached to The Highland Light Infantry because it was mandatory for Indian Army officers to spend their first year in India with a British regiment.

At the end of the year he was posted to The Burma Rifles battalion stationed at Taiping in Malaya. He was a great traveller; in India he used his leaves to trek in the Himalayas and, from Malaya, he visited Japan and came to admire those who would later be his enemies.

At this time the antics of the Rector of Stiffkey (or Stewkey) were much in the news at home and, as Hugh was the son of a Norfolk rector, he was dubbed 'Stooky Seagrim' by his brother officers, and the name stuck. It was a pleasing alliteration if of somewhat dubious origin.

When his battalion returned to Burma he continued his travels in remote places. He would take several Karens from his Company and go to the small mountain villages in the Karenni States for weeks at a time. Thus he learned to love and live with the people whom he was to champion after the Japanese invasion of Burma.

Despite his penchant for living rough in wild hill tracts and his sometimes unconventional military views, he was

* *Grandfather Longlegs* by the late Ian Morrison, Faber & Faber Ltd, London, 1947, gives more detail of Seagrim's life and work among the Karens than is relevant to Ras Pagani's story.

very popular with his brother officers. He was an amusing and witty companion and in no way an 'odd ball' or misfit in the social life of his Regiment.

But he was becoming more and more an admirer of the Karens. He saw their great potential as guerrilla fighters and thought that to subject them to conventional military training, the holding of prepared defensive positions, drilling and wearing boots, was to fail to get the best value out of their natural abilities as mobile guerrilla soldiers. He was skilled at arguing his case but, as a junior officer, was often over-ruled by his seniors.

He also respected the Karens for their strong religious convictions. While not impressed by conventional 'establishment' religious practices among his own race, he set great store by the teachings and language of the Bible, asserting that it was 'the finest literature in the world' and he was never without a Bible during his travels nor, later, during his life with the Karens. This made him a man to respect, in the eyes of the Karens, and a leader whom they could love and follow.

Ras Pagani, a Roman Catholic by up-bringing and conviction, soon found that Hugh Seagrim was interested in many religions and was able to talk, listen or argue about them without giving any impression that he was a 'religious crank'. Ras found his broad views very interesting and they deepened his respect for Seagrim.

Soon after the Japanese declared war in December, 1941, the recruiting of levies from the hill tribes of Burma was accelerated and they were put under the command of H. N. C. Stevenson, an officer of the Burma Frontier Service. Early in 1942 he asked for Seagrim, whom he knew got on well with the Karens, to be seconded to the Burma Levies.

Hugh Seagrim welcomed the appointment as he saw that he would now be able to put into practice the training of Karens as guerrillas, a policy which he had long advocated. Privately, he was also determined that, if the Japanese were to over-run Burma – as they seemed likely to do – he would stay behind enemy lines, living with the Karens.

He went up to Papun and began to recruit Karens, although he was frustrated, to some extent, by the Italian rifles with which they had been issued, especially by the high proportion of faulty ammunition. He cut out all drills and road marches, concentrating on movement through the jungles and on ambush techniques. He also allowed them to fire their rifles from a sitting position as this came naturally to them.

After a few weeks at Papun he moved his headquarters to Pyagawpu, three days' march northwest of Papun, because it was away from the dirt road which led to Papun and which would undoubtedly be used by the Japanese when they advanced on Papun.

In the middle of March, 1942, the Burma Rifles passed through Pyagawpu, on the retreat north to India, and Seagrim was now the only British officer left in the Karenni States. Apart from the Karens with him, he had a few Gurkhas who had been trapped east of the Sittang River when the bridge was blown to prevent it falling into Japanese hands. These men had made their way into the hills where they had been collected by the Karens and brought to Seagrim.

Hugh continued his recruiting and began to organize the resistance movement into area groups. His levy commander in the south was the forest ranger, Saw Willie Saw, who was later to carry Ras Pagani in a bullock cart during his escape into the Karen Hills. In the centre area was Saw Darlington, a tough hard-drinking man. At Pyagawpu Saw Digay, a timber contractor, was Seagrim's lieutenant. Saw Willie Saw commanded nine sections, Saw Darlington twenty and Saw Digay eighteen, each of about eleven men. Every section was supposed to have a Tommy gun with fifty rounds of ammunition, two rifles with thirty rounds each and about four shotguns with forty cartridges each. Some sections had less, some had more, but all were pitifully weak in fire-power against a well-armed enemy and could only expect success by concentrating on hit-and-run tactics, hoping to capture Japanese arms and ammunition in the process.

In mid-April Seagrim decided to march north to try and get in touch with Army Headquarters as he had been out of communication with everyone for several weeks. Assuring the Karens that he would return soon, he set off from Pyagawpu for Mawchi, which he found to be full of Japanese. He skirted round the area, checking each village for Japanese, in the general direction of Taunggyi which he approached towards the end of April. Here he was ambushed by Shan bandits and his companion, Ba Thein, was killed. Seagrim escaped unhurt and headed south again until he reached a jungle village named Mawtudo where he was hidden by two Karen pastors for the next four months, in a hut which they built for him deep in the jungle.

In March, while Seagrim was at Pyagawpu, a force of 150 BIA came to Papun declaring that they were going to take over the administration and demanding that all arms be handed over to them. Only a few rusty shotguns were surrendered. Shortly afterwards the BIA leader, Boh Nya

Na, who had been trained by the Japanese, was ambushed and killed by the Levies while visiting a village south of Papun. This was the signal for his second-in-command, a rogue named Boh Tun Hla, to massacre seventeen Karen elders whom they had detained in Papun. Saw Darlington decided to attack and drive the BIA out of Papun, and Seagrim sent him two Levies under the command of Naik Ah Din. The attack was only partially successful and, although the Levies managed to rescue some Karens from imprisonment in Papun, the BIA retaliated by gathering all the Karens they could catch into a wired compound where machine guns covered them constantly. They also began to molest Karen women and started burning down every village around Papun.

The Levies planned a second attack on Papun but, before it could be carried out, the BIA decamped to Bilin taking with them Karen hostages whom they later murdered. The Levies, infuriated by this, burned down Papun so that the BIA would have nowhere to live should they return. The Karens then moved deep into the jungle, leaving Papun completely deserted for several months.

A state of war now existed between the BIA and the Karens and, by the end of May, 1942, the Levies had driven all BIA and Burmese out of the Salween district. But the Karens now lived in temporary huts in the jungle, short of food because they could not carry out their normal cultivations, and on uneasy guard against punitive expeditions which they were sure would be sent against them.

However, the Japanese, who had by now driven all British and Indian forces from Burma, were in a position to consolidate their hold on the country. They were not impressed by the excesses of the BIA, which reflected

badly on the Japanese, so began, ruthlessly, to comb out
the more undesirable elements and to get the BIA under
control. Consequently the Karenni States were left in
peace for the remainder of 1942.

In December Seagrim moved south to Chawido, a small
village near Pyagawpu, because his hideout at Mawtudo
was very unhealthy and depressing. The Karens would
not allow him to stay in Chawido village in case strangers
spotted him and betrayed him to the Japanese. They built
him a hut in dense jungle a few miles east of the village and
took food and fresh vegetables to him every day.

But, for virtually all Europeans, life in deep jungle is
claustrophobic and depressing, engendering a restless-
ness which often resulted in the making of long and often
pointless and dangerous journeys. Hugh Seagrim was no
exception; he was utterly bored by lack of company and
frustrated by inaction, feeling that his designs for the
Karen resistance were getting nowhere.

After a few weeks he had had enough; he moved back to
Pyagawpu where his spirits were immediately raised by
the companionship of the Karens living there and where
he quickly regained his health.

While he was there Father Calmon came up from
Papun to seek his help. He said that some of the Levies in
the south were behaving badly, using their armed power
to oppress local villagers. Bad feeling had also grown up
between Saw Darlington and Naik Ah Din, and Father
Calmon had, much against his wishes, become involved in
their intrigues against each other.

Seagrim realized that, in his absence, some Levies had
got out of hand. He agreed to call in the Levy Commanders and sort out the troubles. Much relieved, Father

Calmon returned to Papun where, as already related, he found Ras Pagani with Father Loizeau.

During the ten days which Ras Pagani spent with Seagrim at his hut in the jungle the two men became ever closer; Seagrim saw in Ras a man whom he could trust, who had, like himself and the Karens, a strong religious faith and who had already proved himself to be a man of great determination and courage. Ras regarded Seagrim as the most remarkable officer under whom he had ever served and he was willing to help Seagrim's plans in any way he could. But he also realized that Seagrim had been very lonely for several months and saw that his arrival had done much to cheer him up.

Every evening they sat talking round the fire and Seagrim taught Ras much about the Karens and other hill tribes on the east side of Burma. The present inhabitants of Burma had all come originally, he said, from Mongolia, from the wild tracts of country in eastern Tibet or from western China. Probably about four thousand years ago they had started to leave their homes in these inhospitable mountainous regions and, over the course of many centuries, had migrated south to the warmer and more fertile plains of Burma. Some of them – the Chins, Kachins, Shans and Karens – could not entirely shake off their previous existence as mountain dwellers and had settled in the hills which border the rich Burmese plain to the north, east and west.

The Karens, who may have come from China as they are more akin to their Siamese neighbours than to the Burmese who probably came from the Gobi Desert or from eastern Tibet, split their migration into two main streams based on tribal loyalties, the *Sgaw* Karens settling in what are now the Karenni States and the *Pwo* Karens passing west to the Arakan Yomas. Gradually many of them debouched onto the plains, some *Pwo* Karens to the Bassein area and some *Sgaw* Karens to the Irrawaddy delta, but pockets of Karens, especially of the lesser tribes, established themselves in almost every part of Burma, including the Shan States.

As a result of their dispersal over a wide area the Karens were less powerful than the Burmese, who were concentrated on the plains, and the latter despised the Karens, treating them as slaves and often oppressing them. The Karens, however, unlike some of the smaller tribes, refused to be absorbed by the Burmese and retained a strong racial identity and their own customs. The hill tribes, in particular the Karens, held the plains-dwelling Burmese in some contempt, as is the manner of mountain peoples the world over.

The Karens were a happy and honest race, not given to changing their way of life in the forests or in their methods of cultivations, and had peaceful, friendly natures unless aroused to anger.

Gradually, as educational opportunities improved under British rule, many of the more intelligent Karen men entered Government service or trained as doctors, while the women were in great demand as nurses to British children or in hospitals because they were amenable to discipline and had a very high sense of loyalty. This loyalty also made the men desirable as soldiers in the Burma Rifles and Burma Military Police.

It was the conversion of many of them to Christianity, said Seagrim, which interested him. Some Karens were Buddhists, as were the Burmese; others embraced Christianity in one form or another – mainly American

Baptists or Roman Catholics – depending upon their local missionaries who were usually dedicated to the Karens and lived as they did. Some had retained their Animist religion so that it was not unusual to find a Christian village and an Animist village close together in the hills. A few Christians hedged their bets and kept some of their Animist customs, perhaps feeling that they would thus not fall foul of local *nats* (spirit Gods) who lived in the hills, jungles and rivers.

Villages were run by village elders whose decisions were made for the benefit of the whole community, and much of the agricultural work was carried out on the same communal basis. Family ties were very strong, crime was almost unknown and deception in marriage or in business dealings was looked upon with great disfavour.

Sometimes stupid – and often very obstinate – the Karens accepted strangers more slowly, but ultimately more completely, than did the charming, volatile and amusing Burmese on whom no one could place much reliance for long. For centuries the Burmese had lorded it over the Karens and the latter both disliked and distrusted them. Now, in war, with the Burmese backing the Japanese, their fellow-Buddhists, and the Karens remaining loyal to the British, the antagonisms between the two races had deepened.

The Karens' immediate neighbours, the Shans, inhabited hills which were less precipitous and jungle-covered than the Karen hills and, in consequence, lived an easier life and were very easy-going and gentle. Like the Burmese, they were Buddhists so there was not the religious animosity which existed between the Karens and the Burmese. Their rulers were the *Sawbwas* (hereditary princes or rajahs) who governed their tiny realms with a colourful but benign paternalism. (Hugh Seagrim did not live to see that the disruption caused by the war and the departure of the British would cause this even-tempered race to rebel against the Burmese Government and demand independence, raising a Shan Independence Army in 1959. In 1962 General Ne Win staged a military coup in Burma and imprisoned all the *Sawbwas* he was able to catch, others fleeing into exile. By the time the *Sawbwas* were released in 1968, their people had been subjugated and the authority and feudal way of life of their rulers had withered for ever. An amnesty in 1980 allowed those in exile to return to their homes on condition that they accepted the terms of the amnesty.)

Further north, in the cat's-cradle of mountains which bordered Tibet and China, lived the Kachins. They were mainly Animist, brave and cheerful, and were much in demand by the Burma Rifles, Burma Military Police and Burma Frontier Force battalions. They disliked the Burmese intensely (later they also were to raise a Kachin National Army against the Burmese) and, for a time after the war, gave sanctuary to the Burma Communist Party in the wild country adjoining the border with China. The Kachins' homeland gave them virtual immunity from Burmese Government forces, so they retained their independence.

Relations between these hill tribes were, in the main, peaceful. All they asked was to be left alone to live their lives according to their customs but they could be formidable fighters if aroused, in particular the Kachins and Karens, as the Japanese were to find to their cost in the latter stages of the war.

Seagrim then advised Ras on the handling of the Karen Levies, advice which was to prove invaluable to him during the coming months. They discussed the troubles in the south, which Father Calmon had reported a fortnight earlier, and Seagrim decided that Ras should go south, take over command of the whole southern area* and sort out the troubles. As the ex-Burma Rifles Levy commanders were all Naiks (Corporals), Seagrim promoted Ras to Sergeant and gave him written authority for this promotion.

During their talks together Ras Pagani had told Seagrim that his object in escaping had been to travel north and join up with our forces in northern Burma. If successful, he intended to pull every string possible to join 14th Army. By now the Japanese had, to some extent, replaced the Germans as his personal enemies, due to their brutal treatment of his comrades in the railway camps, and he thirsted for revenge.† Therefore, when Saw Po Thin had offered to guide him north to the Arakan Yomas, he had been very tempted to accept as this would have furthered his purpose. However, Saw Po Thin's alternative plan, namely to take him to a British officer who was still fighting the Japanese in the Karenni States, was also attractive. Ras had been a fugitive for several weeks, in constant danger of betrayal and death if recaptured, and he had felt the need of a safe base in which he could rest and set forth again, well prepared, to carry out his original intention.

Hugh Seagrim tried hard to dissuade him from such a hazardous undertaking. He pointed out that the journey would entail traversing many miles of open country which

---

* An area roughly half the size of Norfolk.

† In view of the danger to himself should he be recaptured, it is unlikely that 14th Army would have agreed to his request and he would probably have been sent to a 'non-Japanese' theatre of war.

was inhabited mainly by Burmans, many of whom would be hostile to him. Even if he were to achieve this safely, he still had to cross the Irrawaddy before he could gain the shelter of the Arakan Yomas where there were also Karens who might be willing to guide him north. And the further north he travelled, the greater would be the concentrations of Japanese forces and, consequently, less local guides on whom he could rely. In Seagrim's opinion Ras's chances of breaking safely through the battle zone would be almost nil.

Ras replied that he had already anticipated this last difficulty. He proposed to travel through the Arakan Yomas until he neared Akyab. He felt confident that the Karen guides would find him a boat in which, sailing only by night, he would outflank the Japanese coastal units and join our forces further north.

They argued every aspect of the proposition until Seagrim finally saw that Ras was determined to go once he could do no more for the Karens. Reluctantly agreeing to the plan, he wrote out a long report which Ras was to deliver to Army HQ in the event of his escape being successful, or to destroy if he was in danger of being captured.

They left the matter there and Ras agreed that he would, in the meantime, do everything in his power to help Seagrim with the training and operations of the Karen Levies.

They spent a final day together making preparations for Ras's journey. Although he was sorry to leave Seagrim, Ras felt stimulated by the prospect of his new command and looked forward to the move.

Early the following morning he said goodbye to Seagrim and set off for Pyagawpu to collect a weapon from the hidden stock held there.

As he left the clearing he looked back; Seagrim was still standing by the hut watching him go. To Ras he suddenly seemed a very lonely figure and, at that moment, Ras almost regretted his enthusiasm for setting out on this new adventure. But Seagrim raised his hand in farewell and Ras turned and continued his journey.

He little knew that this was to be the last time he would see Seagrim.

CHAPTER SIX

Pagani's Private Army

Ras Pagani was accompanied by his shadow, Mura, and Seagrim had sent his personal guard of eight men to escort them. They travelled fast and reached Pyagawpu in daylight. Ras and Mura were taken to the Baptist Minister's house beneath which was buried a well-camouflaged cache of weapons including Tommy guns, pistols and both long and short Japanese rifles (the latter normally carried by Japanese mounted troops and a great favourite with the Levies because they were easier to carry and use when travelling in thick jungle). Ras chose a Tommy gun with one drum holding fifty rounds and four box magazines each of twenty rounds. Mura picked a Japanese short rifle and fifty rounds of ammunition.

Meanwhile the Karens, never at a loss to find an excuse for a gathering, had organized a church service to welcome this friend of their revered 'Grandfather Long-legs'. The service was packed with men, women and children and Ras was struck again by the happy faces of this friendly race. He noticed, with surprise, that many of the young girls were fair-skinned and he learned later that they were careful to avoid becoming burnt by the sun because any girl of marriageable age was considered by the Karens to be a beauty if she was fair and also rather plump.

After the service Ras asked for guides to take him south the following day. Every man in the gathering volunteered for the job and the minister had to select a team of eight men. The leader carried a Tommy gun, two were armed with short rifles and two with double-barrelled 12-bore shotguns. The remaining three carried cross-bows, weapons which Ras had not seen before, so he examined them with interest. The stocks were made from hardwood, as were the hand-carved triggers; animal gut provided the strings of the bows and the foot-long bolts were fashioned from bamboo. Each bolt had a sharp pointed end which had been hardened in a fire and, at the rear end, square-cut plantain leaves formed the flight feathers. They were deadly weapons; silent, accurate at fifty paces and with great hitting power. Unlike rifles, they could be made and repaired locally, they did not rust nor did their ammunition suffer in the damp jungles. The Karens had used them for hunting prior to the war and assured Ras that the bolts would pass right through a man. They demonstrated this by firing a bolt at a tree and Ras, using all his strength, found that he was unable to pull the bolt out of the trunk.

As befitted guerrillas, their commissariat was very simple; each man carried a couple of pounds of rice in a cloth which hung from his waist and one man brought a round open basket in which were a few chickens about the size of bantams. Ras asked the minister about water and was told that it was not necessary to carry any as the jungle streams were pure.

Just as they were on the point of leaving, an elephant

was brought out and the guides indicated that Ras should ride on it. He politely declined to do so, because, having observed Seagrim's custom of living like the Karens, he was convinced that, if he was to lead and gain the respect of these hardy mountain fighters, he must show them that an Englishman could do as well, if not better, than them in every aspect of life in the jungle. It says much for his strength of character and clear vision that he was prepared to forego any comfort or privilege which his men did not also enjoy.

They set forth, scrambling up and down jungle-covered hills, forcing their way along overgrown gullies and always moving in a tangle of steaming undergrowth. Sometimes they were beset by leeches; the Karens carried salt in small bags and dabbed these on the leeches until they dropped off. During the march there were times when Ras thought wistfully of that elephant but he had chosen to go on foot and knew he was right in doing so.

Around midday, much to his relief, they stopped by a stream to rest and drink. Now the minister's assurances about the purity of the water became clear and Ras learned another skill of living in the jungle. The Karens dug a hole about a foot deep and the same distance away from the edge of the stream. Water began to seep slowly through the earth into the hole and soon they were able to fill their pots with clear water. Although there was no village nearby and the stream was probably clean anyway, the Karens always took this precaution of filtering the water because there might have been some contamination, such as a dead animal, higher up the stream.

They sat there for a couple of hours, talking and laughing. Although Ras still had to depend to some extent on sign language, he possessed that great ability of all

British soldiers serving in the East to make themselves understood by the natives even though they spoke only a few words of the local language.

When some of the midday heat had gone out of the sun they resumed the march and pushed on for three hours before making camp. Here Ras was initiated into yet another piece of jungle lore, namely, how to cook rice when no water was available. The Karens felled a large green bamboo and cut out of it several complete sections, with joints sealing both ends of each section. They then bored a hole about half an inch in diameter in one end of each section, taking care not to spill the water contained in the bamboo section. The correct amount of rice was poured into each section through the hole which was then plugged with green plantain leaves. A fire was lit, using dry bamboo which gives off terrific heat, and the bamboo sections were put into the heart of the fire for about ten minutes. After this they were taken out and left in the edge of the fire to simmer.

While the rice was being prepared the Karens killed and skinned the chickens. They split them down the backs, opening them up like kippers, and then impaled them on slivers of bamboo which they stuck into the ground very close to the fire. The chicken guts and skins were thrown into the fire so that no wild animals would be attracted to the camp.

For a vegetable to go with the chicken and rice they cut down a plantain (wild banana) tree, stripped it right down to the centre until they had a long, slightly sticky, pole the size of a broomstick. This was eaten raw and tasted rather like cucumber.

After the meal they settled down round the fire. Before he went off into a deep sleep Ras caught glimpses of a clear sky through gaps in the trees above him and was lulled to sleep by noises as the jungle night-life came alive. When he woke at dawn the fire was still alight which surprised him. They drank some water before starting but did not eat any food. Ras learned that it was a Karen custom to have only one meal a day when on the march to avoid overloading their stomachs, and he found that it suited him very well. The routine for the day was the same as the previous day but, when he woke during the night, Ras solved the mystery of the fire: any Karen who woke in the night got up and put more bamboo on it from a pile stacked nearby.

They walked for two more days and, in the evening, arrived at Papun where Ras at once paid a call on Father Loizeau, taking him a present of cheroots. He was the good Father's guest that night and enjoyed a European meal which included a bottle of French white wine. Father Calmon was not there because he was visiting some outlying villages.

They stayed in Papun for three days during which Ras presided over his first court, using one of the few buildings which had not been burned down by the BIA on a previous raid. The accused was an Indian who was charged with selling salt – a vital commodity in the hills – at the exorbitant rate of two and even three rupees per *viss*.* After hearing the evidence and confirming the man's guilt, Ras consulted the Karen elders about a suitable punishment. They advised twenty lashes with a bamboo cane across the buttocks so Ras ordered one of the Levies to carry out this punishment in public. He then gave an order that the price of salt should not exceed one rupee per

* A measurement of weight, 3.6 pounds.

viss in future and that *jāgri* (a coarse brown sugar, like fudge, made from sugar cane) should not be sold for more than half a rupee per *viss*.

After three days they headed south to Kadaingti, a village some thirty-five miles from Papun and the place where Ras had picked up Mura on his journey north to meet Seagrim. He stayed there for nearly a week during which most of the Levy commanders came in to report to him. Among them was Saw Willie Saw who was pleased to see Ras again and glad that he had taken over command of the southern area. He produced a map of the area which Ras studied with a growing feeling that Seagrim had indeed set him a formidable task. Quite apart from his brief to sort out the Levies and plan their operations, the territory over which he would hold sway amounted to several hundred square miles. Twenty miles to the east ran the border with Siam, a very wild area through which the ever-broadening Salween River flowed from north to south. Twelve miles west of the Salween the Yunzalin River divided his territory into two halves and also ran from north to south. To the west lay the wooded country through which he had travelled after leaving Saw Po Thin's house. The whole area was a mixture of jungle, hills, rivers or streams and there were few tracks large enough for a bullock cart to travel, apart from the small road from Bilin to Papun.

However, although the area was difficult to traverse, the very wildness of it ensured that, for the time being, it was free of Japanese troops and, as the BIA had taken a hammering earlier from the Levies, they no longer entered the Karenni States. Both the Japanese and the BIA had been further dissuaded from invading the States by the rumours which Seagrim had deliberately put about, to the effect that two strong battalions of our forces were operating in the hills. The Levies embellished these rumours by adding artillery and even aircraft when passing on these tales. The Japanese, occupied with consolidating their hold on the more populated areas and with the reorganization of the BIA whose past excesses had brought great discredit to the Japanese among the civilian population, were not anxious to add to their burdens until they were ready to do so.

While Ras was at Kadaingti Saw Po Thin came to see him and the usual drinking session took place. The latter was a great champion of the Karens whom he regarded as superior to the Burmese (an opinion fully endorsed by Ras). The Karens alleged that Saw Po Thin paid large sums from his own pocket so that Karen girls could be trained as nurses and bright young men could study in England to become doctors. Hence many of the doctors and nurses in hospitals in Burma were Karens.

During their talks Ras came to realize that Saw Po Thin was the *éminence grise* behind the Karen resistance movement. His work for the Japanese, who required timber for sleepers on the Burma-Siam railway, placed him above suspicion by them and enabled him to move freely about the forests of the Karenni States on his lawful business. Not only did he keep Seagrim and the Levies up-to-date with information about Japanese intentions and troop movements, but he also gave the Levies money, supplies and even arms.*

After about a week at Kadaingti Ras decided to tour his area of command, first to the southern border area and then round the eastern parts of his domain. He took with

* His 'cover' was so good that Ian Morrison in his book, *Grandfather Longlegs*, does not mention him at all.

him Naik Ah Din, a section of Ah Din's men whom Ras
personally selected, the six 'cut-off' Gurkhas and Lance
Naik Mura. Before starting Ras was careful to leave a plan
of his proposed itinerary in case any trouble should blow
up in his absence.

They travelled south for several days until they had
reached the limits of his territory. Here the country was
more open, cultivation being broken up by occasional
thickets of bamboo and plantain. Consequently the
villages were an easy prey for marauding BIA forces and
the inhabitants lived mainly in temporary shelters in
patches of jungle rather than risk being surprised in their
villages by the BIA who had already burned some to the
ground.

The routine for each day's journey was as already
described but Ras tried to spend at least one day in each
camp so that he could meet Levies and Karen elders. The
only snag about this leisurely progress was that the
Karens organized a drinking session nearly every night.
Consequently Ras, who was no drinker, set off each day
with a thick head which was only cured by several hours of
marching. Nevertheless, it was a happy time for him; he
had his own command and was much cheered by the
enthusiasm with which the local people welcomed him.
The arrangements for each stop and the provision of
guides for each march he left to Ah Din as this was his area
of operations and he knew it well.

When Ras felt that he had done as much as he could in
the south, he gave orders for the party to move to the
eastern area. They crossed the Yunzalin River and
plunged into jungle-covered hills.

The marches through the hills, although physically
exhausting because many of the ranges ran up to six or

seven thousand feet and were steep and covered with jungle trees or bamboo, were a joy to Ras. After his life in the squalid prison camps the forests restored to him a sense of freedom which was as heady as wine. Because there was no danger of attack by the Japanese or BIA in these remote regions, he was able to enjoy the beauty of his surroundings. Sometimes they walked in deep shade, shafts of sunlight occasionally piercing the gloom and lighting up clouds of yellow butterflies which carpeted damp patches on the paths and rose at their approach to drift away among the trees like showers of golden leaves. In the tree canopy above, unseen monkeys crashed through the boughs or sat uttering mournful cries as they peered down at these human invaders of their sanctuary.

The nights in the hills were cool so Ras and his men lay round a fire after their meal, listening idly to the sounds of the jungle creatures before falling into deep sleep. If there was a moon, the forest took on a ghostly sheen, a background to the flickering fireflies. With the coming of dawn a damp chill mist arose, heralded by the shrill crowing of jungle fowl and followed by the insect chorus as the rising sun warmed the glades.

For three days they travelled through these hills until at last they began to descend to the Salween River which here formed the border with Siam. A cluster of huts clung to the river bank and here they found the local commander (whose name Ras has forgotten). He was not one of the Levies and was, in fact, little more than a *dacoit** who, with his gang of twenty men, carried out raids into both Siam and Burma. He had acquired large quantities of arms and ammunition but these he would not give to

* Highway robber.

the Karens, only selling them in exchange for gold and jewellery which he put in his own pocket. He was not popular among local people but they tolerated him because he was a Karen whose father and brother had been murdered by the Japanese, so the Karens were confident that he would never betray the Levies to the Japanese or BIA.

He was delighted with the visit by Ras as it gave him additional standing in the eyes of the local population. He threw a magnificent party for them, including a bevy of Siamese dancing girls from over the border and the Levies had to stay there for two days to recover from these excesses.

At last, bidding farewell to their host, who had provided them with guides, they headed north and fought their way through a very wild area of mountains and jungles. Occasionally they came across hamlets where the people were growing hill rice. This entailed clearing and burning off an area of jungle. As only one crop of rice could be harvested and the area then had to lie fallow for seven years, the following year the process was carried out in other nearby areas of jungle. It was a custom which was wasteful in timber and led eventually to soil erosion on the hillsides.* After four years the villagers usually moved to another site, mainly for reasons of hygiene as Ras learned to his cost when they came to a village, perched on a steep hillside, whose inhabitants had decided to extend their stay to a fifth year. As they approached the houses their legs were smothered in fleas which swarmed up from the contaminated ground so they hastily decided not to stay there but to cross the Siamese border to a place named

* Called *Taungya* cultivation by the Karens.

Hot.* This was a large village containing several sub-stantial wooden houses. It was inhabited almost entirely by Karens who had, in the past, fled from persecution by the Burmese, and had been allowed to settle there by the Siamese. The whole area was extremely remote and was part of what is now known as the 'golden triangle', an opium-growing centre beyond the control of the Siamese police and virtually without the law.

Ras was taken to what the locals proudly called a 'travellers' rest-house' where he slept in luxury in a proper bed with sheets and a mosquito net. His visit caused quite a stir as apparently none of the villagers had ever before set eyes on a white man and many from surrounding villages also poured in to see him. He had to stay for three days, at the insistence of his hosts, and the inevitable dinner parties and drinking sessions took place each night. By the end of three days Ras felt that he had shaken the hand of every man and woman within twenty miles. It was a 'Shangri-la' world at that time, before it acquired its evil reputation for supplying the western world with drugs, and Ras was sorry to leave it but he had other duties to carry out and his liver was beginning to feel the strain of a succession of convivial nights.

They re-crossed the border at Dagwin and headed back to Kadaingti, a journey which lasted a week and took them through jungle-covered mountains.

During the journey he had got to know many of the Levies and had formed his opinion of the qualities and weaknesses of the section commanders. Saw Darlington, a very tough character whose rather foul pipe was seldom out of his mouth, was always itching to attack the

---

* Not to be confused with the better known village of Hot, which lies about 40 miles south-west of Chieng-Mai, in Siam.

Japanese and BIA. He was sometimes at odds with his fellow commanders but his anger seldom lasted and, before long, he was laughing again, especially at his own jokes. A bad squint in one eye did nothing to deter him from being an ardent ladies' man nor to make him unattractive in their eyes. He had previously been in the Burma Military Police and was not only trustworthy but, during the coming weeks, proved himself to be courageous in battle. Ras felt a strange affinity with his piratical-looking leader – perhaps seeing something of himself in the man's character.

Saw Willie Saw, an ex-forest ranger, had a totally different personality to Darlington. He was well-educated and spoke good English – as did his wife and two daughters – and was always cool and calculating, even in moments of crisis. His area was nearest to the Japanese and BIA posts at Thaton and Bilin so he was always the first to know of any threat to the Karens or of the arrival of 'strangers' in the hills. Ras regarded him as a personal friend and had implicit trust in him.

Ah Din, although very loyal to Ras, had to be watched carefully. He had, in the past, quarrelled bitterly with Saw Darlington and Gyaw Lai and Ras suspected that, if left to his own devices, he would probably have become little better than an armed *dacoit*, oppressing the Karen villagers as well as fighting the enemy. He had been detached from Seagrim's personal bodyguard to come with Ras and possibly considered himself superior to the other commanders. Ras thought that he had a slight inferiority complex which led to his aggressiveness to his fellows, but he later found him to be brave in action to the point of recklessness.

The last section commander, Naik Gyaw Lai, was a

very cool and quiet young man who had served in the Burma Rifles. But his calmness concealed a spirit of steel, as he was to display in action against the Japanese at Papun. Ras both liked and trusted him but decided to keep him away from the prickly Ah Din by posting him to the Salween River area. There is no record of him being killed or captured by the Japanese, like so many of his comrades, so it may be that, when the Japanese swarmed into the hills, Gyaw Lai just skipped over the border into Siam and lay low until they had gone.

Apart from the commanders, Ras had close links with two other Karens. First, Lance Naik Mura, who had attached himself to Ras as orderly, bodyguard and general factotum – even to the extent of tasting Ras's food if anyone other than himself had cooked it. He had served in the Burma Rifles and was a Kachin from Assam. He spoke only Burmese and Hindi but he and Ras managed to understand each other without difficulty. He proved to be selflessly loyal to Ras, as will be seen later in the story. Second, an intelligent young Karen from Papun, Saw Po Hla, who was only in his early teens but was full of daring and initiative. He was an orphan as his parents had been murdered by the BIA when they had occupied Papun the previous year and had taken hostage many of the elders whom they later killed. His speciality was to visit Thaton and villages on the plains to gather information about Japanese and BIA dispositions and intentions, often at great personal risk. Later, when Ras had left the Karenni States, Saw Po Hla attached himself to Seagrim and performed a similar service. He will appear again later in the story.

Also, during his travels, Ras had given much thought to the implementation of Seagrim's instructions to 'sort out

R.A.S. Pagani aged about 19 as a Private Soldier in
The East Surrey Regiment, 1934.

Pagani aged 13½ in page-boy's uniform.

Pagani aged about 17.

(Left) H.P. Seagrim, 1936. *(Below)* The village sign at Whissonsett, Norfolk, commemorating Lt-Colonel Derek Seagrim VC and Major Hugh Seagrim GC, DSO, MBE.

Father Jean Edouard Calmon.

Father Paul Gaston Loizeau at his ordination, July, 1900.

The church at Pyagawpu.

Saw Darlington.   Lieutenant Motoichi Inoue.

Father Loizeau celebrating Mass with the Karens, 1942.

Typical country in the Salween district.

The Salween where it flows through the Karen country.

The country near Komupwado.

Operation Character; a Lysander landing on an improvised strip in the Karen Hills.

Major H.P. Seagrim, GC, DSO, MBE.

R.A.S. Pagani, MM, aged 30, on his release from captivity, 1945.

Pagani's cell in the New Law Courts.

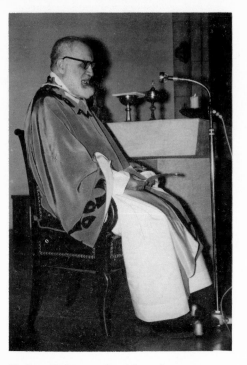

Father Calmon after his retirement, 1968.

An NCO of the Kempeitai, drawn by Ronald Searle, also a prisoner of the Japanese. (Copyright © 1986, Ronald Searle)

R.A.S. Pagani, MM, aged 72, 1987.

the troubles between Levy commanders'. By the time he
had returned to Kadaingti he knew the commanders well
and had made up his mind how best to carry out
Seagrim's orders. First, he announced to the Levies that
he would make Kadaingti his headquarters and would
split the southern area into smaller, well-defined,
commands. Ah Din would be responsible for Kadaingti
and the villages immediately around it but would himself
live in Kadaingti and thus under Ras's eye. As the main
friction had been between Ah Din and Naik Gyaw Lai,
Ras posted the latter to the eastern area, near the Salween,
and Naik Saw Darlington, another commander who had
caused trouble in the past, he sent to command the Papun
area. To Saw Willie Saw, whom he could trust implicitly,
he gave an area to the south-west which included the more
outlying villages of Kadaingti. Each Levy commander
was given clear orders concerning the extent of the area
under his command and of the conduct which Ras
expected him to observe in that area. He got the
impression that they were quite happy with this reorganization and were even relieved that they now knew
exactly where they stood.

Ras Pagani, having thus firmly asserted the authority
which Seagrim had given him, felt that he was in a strong
position in the Levies and could now concentrate on
carrying out Seagrim's instructions regarding operations
by the Levies. He was confident that all Levy commanders had 'got the message' and that no further friction
would arise among them, nor any abuse of their power vis
à vis the civilians in the areas over which they had control.

During his absence on tour there had been no trouble in
the area except for the usual harassment of border villages
by gangs of BIA. Ras now gave orders to the occupants of

these villages to withdraw north to the hill villages where they could be more easily protected, and this was quickly accomplished. But he had a feeling that they could soon expect trouble from the Japanese and/or the BIA and it would be vital then that harmony and comradeship should prevail between Levy commanders.

His intuition was to prove correct; within two weeks of his reorganization the Levies would find themselves in action against their enemies.

CHAPTER SEVEN

The Enemy Closes In

Barely ten days after Ras had issued his orders for the reorganization of the Levies, the tranquillity of their life in the Karenni States was threatened.

A runner arrived with the disturbing news that a small force of BIA had attacked one of the border villages in the south and, after murdering some men and raping any women whom they could seize, had set it on fire. The messenger added that they were now moving north up the road towards Kadaingti.

Ras called out his and Ah Din's sections and they set off southwards to intercept the enemy. The following day they sighted them; fifteen men, all armed and wearing BIA arm bands, moving up the road.

Hurriedly Ras selected a suitable ambush position and deployed his sections. Silent and motionless they waited until, at last, the BIA men came into view, sauntering carelessly along the road and talking loudly, apparently confident that they were safe. Ras let them into the ambush area and then opened fire at point blank range: the sections followed suit and the BIA fell like ninepins.

With a shout Ras launched himself at them, closely followed by the Karens. After a short struggle they captured the only five who had survived the initial bursts of fire, ten men having been killed immediately. None of the Karens had received even a scratch. There could be no question of allowing the captured men to return to the plains so Ras held a court, found them guilty of rape and murder, and sentenced them to death by firing squad. There was no shortage of volunteers for the execution which was carried out after Ras had made the culprits dig their own graves in order to save his men the exertion of digging. After the graves had been filled in the sections collected fifteen rifles and two pistols, together with their ammunition, and also the BIA armbands which Ras thought might be useful if he had to send Levies on spying missions outside the Karenni States. The captured weapons and ammunition constituted a considerable extra load so they called in on Saw Willie Saw at Molopa where they hid the weapons and spent the night.

The following day they returned to Kadaingti for a well-earned sleep and wash. Lance Naik Mura, who, in addition to acting as bodyguard to Ras, had extended his duties to washing Ras's clothes, and to preparing his food, now produced from somewhere a civilian-type *topee* – known as a Bombay bowler – which he considered to be an essential mark of a *sahib*. But, in Ras Pagani's experience, they were nowadays more often worn by Eurasians. A mixture of European parentage himself, Ras always had a soft spot for the Eurasian whom he thought had a very raw deal in life in India, not accepted by Indians, barely tolerated by Europeans, and confined socially and in their work to limited areas such as the Railways and Posts and Telegraphs. Having lived as a coolie under his Japanese captors his sympathies for the Eurasians had become even more sharpened.

Two days later danger threatened them again. A report came in to Ras that two Burmans were travelling from village to village with a bullock cart full of salt which they were trying to sell at two rupees a *viss*. But they were also asking if anyone had two white elephants* for sale, or if anyone knew where there were two. They were offering the whole cartload of salt in exchange for the beasts. They had, unwisely, called on Saw Willie Saw at his home in Molopa. Naturally suspicious of all Burmans, especially as few had dared to enter the Karen-dominated hill areas for some months, and realizing that the offer of a load of salt in exchange for such valuable animals was ludicrous, he decided to play along with them to try and find out more of their motives. It did not take him long to deduce that the two white elephants were, in fact, Seagrim and Pagani, and that he was being bribed to betray them. He therefore told them that he knew of only one white elephant and that the following day he would guide them to the owner, and, if necessary, assist in its capture. He asked them to be his guests for the night and meanwhile sent a runner to warn Ras that he was going to bring them to Kadaingti the next day. He kept up a pretence of having no suspicions of their real motives and the following day took them to the headman of Kadaingti, who also welcomed them.

Suddenly, Ras, Mura and two Gurkhas, all armed to the teeth, strode into the headman's house. The Burmans were thrown quite off-balance by their sudden appearance, as Ras had intended they should be. He shook each

* Not really white, more grey-pink. Rare and valuable, especially in Siam where they are used by Royalty.

man warmly by the hand and one of them bowed twice to him so Ras instantly suspected that the man was a Japanese. To make sure he suddenly bellowed 'Kiotski'* at him. Startled out of his wits the man sprang rigidly to attention so that Ras knew for certain that he was a Japanese soldier, probably of the notorious *Kempeitai*.

As they were in civilian clothes and could be regarded as spies, Ras was quite entitled to execute them. Indeed, he had no alternative; they could not possibly be released – the Karens would have killed them if he had done so – and he could not afford to encumber himself with dangerous prisoners. He therefore told Ah Din to take them out and shoot them. For a fleeting moment he wondered whether he himself was fast becoming as ruthless as the Japanese but, after thinking back to the sadistic ill-treatment meted out by the Japanese to his comrades in the prison camps, he could find no mercy in his heart for these men. His was a savage war against a bestial enemy; his survival depended on being at least as cunning and ruthless as the Japanese, without indulging in their more loathsome practices of torture.

The next day Ras received a report that a force of fifty Japanese and twenty-five BIA had left Bilin and was travelling along the road to Papun. They were taking with them several Karen elders whom they had collected on the way, as hostages and as an insurance against attack by the Levies.

Ras immediately sent out runners to all the villages on the road which lay ahead of this force to tell the inhabitants to take to the jungle and to leave no food or livestock in the villages. He sent the same warning to Naik Saw Darling-

---

* Japanese command – 'Kiotsukē' – 'Stand to attention!'

ton at Papun, telling him on no account to attack this strong enemy force unless Ras ordered him to do so.

Then, calling out four sections, he set out to cover the thirty-five miles to Papun. He had no intention of making a frontal attack against trained and well-armed Japanese troops who, in any case, outnumbered his Levies, as this would have been quite contrary to Seagrim's policy of using the Levies in a guerrilla role. Their job was to hit the enemy hard and fast and then to melt away before he could mount a counter-attack, but Ras hoped that, by a show of strength in the night, he might scare the enemy into leaving Papun, especially as they would be limited to the food and ammunition which they had been able to carry and their supply line to Bilin was long and liable to ambush by the Levies.

By carrying out a forced march he reached the outskirts of Papun just before dusk the following day only to find that the enemy had beaten him to it and were now encamped in Papun itself, around the crossroads.

After their strenuous march he and his men needed food and rest so he decided to take no action until the following night. At dawn the next day, taking great care that the enemy did not see him, he reconnoitred the area and made his plan. He decided to wait until midnight, at which time he guessed that most of the enemy would be asleep, and then to create, by gunfire, as much mayhem and confusion as possible in a short time, withdrawing to his present position to regroup in safety as soon as the enemy began to react strongly.

He decided to lead two sections in an attack along the Bilin-Papun road, which ran from north-east to south-west. The other two sections, under Naik Gyaw Lai, were to take up a position near Father Calmon's house and attack simultaneously from the Kadaingti-Papun road, which ran north to south. The Japanese camp would thus be subjected to fire from two directions at once and, as the directions of attack were almost at right-angles to each other, there would be no danger of the Levies firing on each other in the darkness.

As soon as it was dark they moved cautiously forward and by 10 pm had reached positions which overlooked Papun and the enemy camp. Here they waited quietly, confident that they would be able to surprise the enemy and inflict casualties on them.

Excitement mounted among the waiting men as, gradually, lights were extinguished and the Japanese camp became silent. Then, as so often happens when an attack has been carefully planned, an unforeseen and trivial incident now threw a spanner in the works; soon after 11 pm they heard voices and an armed party of drunken BIA men came laughing and shouting down the Bilin road.

It was a moment for quick decisions; Ras had no idea why they were there or where they were going as there were no villages along the road for the next eight miles, but he felt certain that they did not know that the Levies were near or they would not have made so much noise. All his sections were in position, ready to attack, and he could not now afford to delay his attack until midnight because, by then, these BIA men would be behind him during his attack and withdrawal.

He waited until they were within about twenty yards and then, flanked by Ah Din and Mura, stepped out into the road, gave a shout to check the BIA, and pressed the trigger of his Tommy gun on which he had fitted a drum magazine of fifty rounds.

Nothing happened! For a second there was dead silence as he had told the Levies not to open fire until he did. Luckily for him, the BIA, startled by his shout, also froze into immobility, giving Ras time to whip off the drum magazine (which had been knocked out of its slide at some time), ram in a box magazine and open fire, closely followed by Ah Din and Mura.

All this happened in a matter of seconds, but to Ras the shock of finding that his gun would not fire when the enemy were only a few yards away made the delay seem minutes long. They killed several BIA and the remainder ran back along the road to Papun. Gyaw Lai and his sections, hearing the firing, also opened up on the Japanese camp and gave it all they had for about five minutes.

Then the Japanese, never sluggards at getting into action, replied with mortars which they had wisely set up during daylight hours to fire on likely lines of attack along the roads. Mortar bombs began to burst quite close to Ras, and the untrained Levy recruits, who had not previously experienced bombardment, ran back in panic. But the Gurkhas and ex-Burma Rifles men stood fast with him, calmly firing on the Japanese camp. The Japanese, now thoroughly alerted, brought their machine-guns and rifles into action so Ras deemed it wise to break off the action and retire to the assembly area before any of his men could be killed or wounded.

They reached the rendezvous without any difficulty, collecting up on the way those Karens who had run back, and Gyaw Lai soon joined them with his sections. They set off in the dark to put more ground between themselves and the Japanese, who continued to fire for some time, and then laid up until dawn.

As soon as it was light they moved on to a hiding place near Saw Darlington's village where they stayed for a week while Ras sent out spies to pick up information about the success of their attack. Reports soon came into him that the Japanese and BIA had both suffered casualties and, having run out of food and most of their ammunition, were packing up and moving back to Bilin. So the object of the attack had been achieved and, more importantly, no Levies had been killed or wounded.

While they were staying with Saw Darlington, Father Calmon came to visit Ras. He was very frightened about the increasing activity of the Japanese and BIA in the Karen Hills. He suggested to Ras that they should give themselves up to the Japanese in exchange for a promise that the Japanese would leave the Karens in peace.

Ras was furious and gave Father Calmon a piece of his mind. Did Father Calmon, he asked, really believe that one could make any treaty with the Japanese which the latter would honour? He himself had had plenty of experience of their methods and had found them to be sadistic bullies to whom any sign of weakness was an invitation to increased brutality. The Karens, far from being left in peace, would be tortured and massacred until they were finally crushed and too terrified to resist. Was that what Father Calmon wanted for them, he demanded? And what about Seagrim and the Levies; was Father Calmon prepared to betray them, as he would surely be made to do once the Japanese had laid their hands on him?

Poor Father Calmon looked very unhappy during Ras's attack on him. He was thinking only of saving his flock from the cruelties of the Japanese. (In fact, he gave himself up a few months later when the Japanese, who had long

suspected him of involvement with the resistance movement, had issued threats of dire reprisals against the
Karens if he did not surrender himself).

For Ras Pagani the matter was a clear-cut military one;
apart from the fact that he could not surrender himself
because he would be executed as an escaped PoW, he saw
the situation from a soldier's point of view. His country
was at war with the Japanese; Seagrim had given him
orders to fight them. This he intended to do to the best of
his abilities – indeed, he had escaped at great personal risk
for this very purpose. He was at war with the Japanese; in
war people were killed if they took part in it. It was as
simple as that.

He made his attitude plain to Father Calmon and the
latter departed sadly. Ras never saw him again.

Ras now decided that, instead of returning to
Kadaingti, he would go north to Pyagawpu, find Seagrim
and tell him about the situation in the south and how the
threat from the enemy was increasing daily.

During the journey he would visit every village between
Papun and Pyagawpu, warn the elders that the Japanese
were likely to come to the Karen hills in force in the near
future, and advise them to take to the jungles with all their
food and livestock.

He sent the Levies back to Kadaingti and took with him
only Mura and his section of Gurkhas. He passed through
Papun, now empty of the enemy, but where he saw Father
Loizeau for a few minutes, and then pushed on north,
arriving in Pyagawpu twelve days later. Here he met the
Baptist minister who told him that there had recently
been considerable movement of Japanese troops along the
Mawchi road, a force of seventy Japanese had come from
Papun to Pyagawpu a week previously and had searched

the village for English soldiers, and that Seagrim had had to go into hiding again. The Minister did not know where Seagrim had gone and, although Ras questioned many Karens, none of them knew either, or, if they did, were not willing to divulge Seagrim's whereabouts even to Ras.

Ras accepted this philosophically because he knew, from his talks with Seagrim, that when the latter went into hiding he made sure that only one or two Karens knew even the rough area where he would be living. His view was that, quite apart from his own security, if too many Karens knew where he was and one of them was betrayed, the man might be subjected to prolonged and hideous tortures to make him reveal the hideout. If the Karens did not know then they could not tell the Japanese and their obvious ignorance under interrogation might convince the Japanese of their innocence and spare them from the more extreme forms of torture.

After hanging about for three or four days Ras realized that he was not going to find Seagrim and that he now had to decide what he was going to do. The options were few, all of them dangerous and some unsatisfactory.

He could return to Kadaingti but he felt that he had carried out Seagrim's orders to reorganize the Levies there and they could now get on with it. They lived in the country and knew it well, whereas he stuck out like a sore thumb and might become a liability to them if they had, under increasing enemy pressure, to be responsible for hiding him as well as looking after themselves and their families.

He could go into hiding in the Pyagawpu area and hope that, one day, he would be re-united with Seagrim. But this might not be for a long time because the Japanese, through their spies, had obviously seen through Seagrim's deliberate rumours of strong British forces still holding out in the Karenni States and were now preparing to close in from both north and south. The Japanese soldier and the Burman whom Ras had executed at Kadaingti proved that the enemy knew that he and Seagrim were in the Karen hills and Ras felt that they might eventually catch him and return him to 18 Km Camp to be shot. There seemed no future in hiding here where his presence would not further any operations and where he might even endanger the lives of local Karens, especially as the Japanese had now re-occupied Papun and had already visited Pyagawpu in strength.

He was of no use to Seagrim now if he could not find him: nor could Seagrim help him.

After much careful thought he returned to his original plan, namely to try and reach our forces in northern Burma, to tell them what was happening to prisoners of war in Japanese hands, to deliver Seagrim's report to 14th Army H.Q. and to put them in the picture about the present situation in the Karenni States. After that he would be able to continue fighting the Japanese under the more conventional wing of 14th Army. He felt that this was important as he held valuable information and it was his duty to try to deliver it.

Nevertheless, it was an agonizing decision to make. He remembered only too clearly the lonely figure of Hugh Seagrim as he had last seen him before setting out for Pyagawpu in December. He loved and admired Seagrim who had given him so much friendship and inspiration and, although convinced he was doing the right thing, he hated the thought of going away without seeing Seagrim or even being able to get a message to him.

But, having made the decision, he began to make preparations for the journey. Three times during this war fortune had smiled on him; coming home from Dunkirk, getting out of Singapore and escaping from 18 Km Camp. He was certain that God had protected him on these occasions; now he needed just one more slice of luck to get him to the Karens who lived in the Arakan Yomas, across the Irrawaddy River. After that he would be in God's hands and he was confident that he would reach our forces.

But that fickle lady, luck, was to turn her face from him at this fourth request for her favours. His journey was to lead him to the very gates of Hell and almost to cost him his life and his sanity.

CHAPTER EIGHT

The Japanese Begin the Hunt for Seagrim

We must now leave Ras Pagani, preparing himself for his dangerous journey north, and look back to see how Seagrim had fared after he had sent Ras south, just before Christmas, 1942, to sort out the troubles which had arisen between Levy commanders.

It is not within the scope of this book to recount in detail the exploits of this remarkable officer except in so far as they affect Pagani's story.

However, from early December, 1942, until early March, 1943, the stories of the two men are intertwined; what happened to Seagrim was, to some extent, responsible for Pagani's decision to try to reach our forces in northern Burma. Therefore, it is to Morrison's account that we must now turn in order to clarify the Seagrim/Pagani story.

Ian Morrison, a war correspondent with 14th Army, and author of several books, was on the spot when the Japanese surrendered in 1945. He was able to move freely about the Karenni States and southern Burma, to question Japanese PoWs and Burmans who had held office under the Japanese, to study Japanese reports and records, and to interview many leading Karens who had known Seagrim and Pagani. His experience and skill in collecting and correlating evidence enabled him to write his book in great detail.

Many of the leaders of the early resistance – Seagrim himself, Ah Din and several others – had been executed by the Japanese on 2 September, 1944. Others had been imprisoned outside the Karenni States so knew little of events there after 1943; some had died in prison, a few had escaped from their captors and had rejoined the resistance during the last months of the war.

But there were many Karens who were able to give Morrison accounts of their lives under the Japanese and it was from their tales that he was able to piece together the story of Seagrim and the Karen resistance. Pagani, the Karens believed, had been killed near Allanmyo while trying to cross the Irrawaddy River. They spoke with sadness of his death, because they admired him for his firm leadership and outstanding courage in battle. It was not until Morrison had returned to England, his book almost ready for publication, that he discovered that Pagani had survived. He was just in time to add an appendix to the book which told Pagani's story very briefly.

January, and the first half of February, 1943, had passed more quietly for Hugh Seagrim than it had for Pagani in the south.

But then reports of Japanese troop movements began to reach Seagrim and, towards the end of February, the peacefulness of his life was abruptly shattered. A runner hammered on the door of Ta Roe, a well-to-do cultivator and an old friend of Seagrim, in the early hours of 25 February, 1943. Ta Roe lived in the small village of Chawido, just north of Pyagawpu.

As soon as the messenger had regained his breath he gasped out that a friend of Ta Roe's, who lived in a village midway between Papun and Pyagawpu, had sent him urgently to warn Ta Roe that a force of Japanese was moving by night from Papun to Pyagawpu. He added that, although he had run throughout the night, the Japanese were probably not far behind him.

Ta Roe's immediate thought was that he must save Seagrim, who was living in Pyagawpu, and he prayed that he was not already too late to do so. Hurriedly dressing, he got out one of his elephants and set off in the dark for Pyagawpu at the animal's best speed.

On arrival he woke Seagrim and the Karens who were with him; hastily gathering up their few belongings and making sure that they had left no tell-tale signs of their stay in Pyagawpu, Seagrim led his men away quickly and headed for his original jungle hideout a few miles east of Chawido. The brave Ta Roe remained in Pyagawpu to face the Japanese.

Seagrim had left in the nick of time; a bare half hour after his departure a force of seventy Japanese stormed into the village. They rounded up all the inhabitants, including Ta Roe, and grilled them about the presence of English soldiers in the area around Pyagawpu. They said that they had information that at least two thousand British soldiers were operating in the hills and being supplied by parachute drops from India. They made it clear that the penalty for helping or hiding these soldiers, or for giving false information to the Japanese, was death. They demanded immediate information about the soldiers.

The Karens here had not previously had any contact with the Japanese but tales of the latter's cruelties had preceded them and the villagers were struck dumb with fear. It was indeed fortunate that Ta Roe was there to speak for them before any villager could break down and blurt out the truth. Calmly he told the Japanese officer that there were no British soldiers in Pyagawpu, nor had he heard of any being in the hills. He suggested that the Japanese should search the village for, surely, he added, they would be certain of finding some trace if two thousand soldiers had been there. The villagers, rallied by his calm leadership, echoed his denials and co-operated with the Japanese in combing through the village.

They searched for an hour but found no trace of English soldiers. However, they were still suspicious and, partly to save their 'face', ordered Ta Roe and two village elders to return with them to Papun for further questioning. Before leaving, Ta Roe managed to whisper to a trusted elder, who was remaining in the village, that Seagrim's hiding place was not now safe enough and that he must be moved at once into the mountainous jungle region north-west of Pyagawpu. The elder promised to do this as soon as the Japanese had left the village.

The three-day march to Papun was a miserable one for Ta Roe and his companions as they feared for their lives. On arrival, another Japanese officer interrogated them about English soldiers around Pyagawpu. They repeated their denials with firmness. Eventually, the Japanese either believed them or saw that they were getting nowhere with these Karens, and said that they could now return to Pyagawpu, but added that they would be held personally responsible with their lives if there was any trouble in future in the Pyagawpu area. Assuring the

Japanese of their co-operation in future, Ta Roe and the elders left Papun feeling that they were safe for the moment.

Reaching Pyagawpu three days later, Ta Roe was delighted to find that the faithful elder had already moved Seagrim and his men to a hiding place in the jungle near to a small village named Payasedo, some twenty odd miles west of Pyagawpu. The elder confirmed that he had taken them there himself and that no other Karens in Pyagawpu or Chawido knew where Seagrim had been hidden.

Ta Roe, telling the elder to forget where he had hidden Seagrim, assumed full responsibility for Seagrim's safety and, returning to Chawido, loaded up an elephant with supplies which he then took to the hiding place. For the next few months Seagrim remained there, supplied once a month by Ta Roe himself, while 700 Japanese occupied Papun and scoured the Karen hills for 'the English soldiers'.

These events occurred just before Ras returned to Pyagawpu; in fact, he was lucky that, after leaving Saw Darlington and calling on Father Loizeau for a few minutes in Papun, he had decided to visit all the hill villages between Papun and Pyagawpu, to warn them to expect the Japanese at any moment and to be prepared to take to the jungle with their food stocks and animals. Had he not done this, he might well have bumped into the Japanese force during his journey to Pyagawpu and been captured.

But, with the security clamp-down imposed by Ta Roe, it was not surprising that Ras was unable to find Seagrim nor to get any news of his whereabouts from Karens in Pyagawpu. All they could tell him was that Seagrim had left in great haste just before dawn a week earlier and they had no idea where he had gone. Ras did not know Ta Roe, who had returned to Chawido before Ras reached Pyagawpu. Had he known him, or had Ta Roe been aware that he had returned to Pyagawpu, perhaps Ras would have been taken to join Seagrim. However, this did not take place and Ras now had to make his own decisions.

The visit in strength by the Japanese to such a small village as Pyagawpu, following so closely on their occupation of Papun, confirmed his view that the Karenni States were becoming very dangerous for him – as well as for local Karens if he were to be killed or captured – and it strengthened his resolve to set out for northern Burma without delay. Apart from the fact that he felt it his duty to try and reach our forces in the north, he knew that he could be of little help to the Karens in this new and dangerous situation and might even be a liability to them.

He was under no illusions concerning the great dangers of the journey ahead but he felt that God would continue to protect him and anything was better than hanging about in the Karen hills awaiting inevitable capture and execution.

CHAPTER NINE

A Disastrous Journey

For three days they travelled north, moving at night and
lying up in Karen villages by day. Ras Pagani, with Mura
and the Gurkhas, were passed from village to village by
guides supplied by Karen elders for each stage of the
journey.

They kept well clear of Mawchi, which was full of
Japanese troops, and then turned north-west. After
marching for several days they began to descend through
the foothills east of the Sittang River, struggling with
difficulty through dense jungle on the hill slopes. To the
west the Sittang flowed south through an open plain about
fifteen miles wide which consisted mainly of dry *padi*
fields. Keeping well south of Toungoo and skirting all
villages so that no Burmese villagers should see them, they
moved silently across the plain until they reached the east
bank of the Sittang River. After a short delay the guides
produced a boat and ferried them across the river. They
continued for three or four miles until they came to the
road and railway which ran north from Rangoon to
Toungoo. There was no traffic at this time of night so,

after a quick reconnaissance to check whether there were any Japanese posts or patrols on the line, they crossed both these obstacles and hurried on for an hour or so, entering the Pegu Yomas just as dawn was breaking.

The hills here were about a thousand feet high and were heavily forested with teak, bamboo and plantain so they felt safe from prying eyes. They soon reached a Karen village where they fed and slept until darkness fell. Over the next few days they were guided by Karens from one village to another until, at last, they reached the western edge of the Yomas.

Ahead of them now a plain stretched as far as the eye could see, endless dry *padi* fields with small villages dotted about them. These hamlets nestled in clumps of mango trees, bamboo and palms and Ras knew that they would be inhabited mainly by Burmese. Once he had crossed the Irrawaddy River and gained the Arakan Yomas he would be with Karens again. Apart from occasional patches of rough ground and hillocks on which grew dense thorny scrub, there were few places where concealment was possible in daylight for such a large party as he had with him. He therefore decided to send the Gurkhas back to the Karen hills with the guides. He wrote chits for them, saying that they had been cut off in battle and had continued to fight the Japanese under his command. He felt that if and when they eventually rejoined our forces they would be received with honour and no charges of desertion from their original units would be levelled at them.

Mura had insisted on staying with Ras so the two of them now set out alone on the next – and most dangerous – stage of their journey. They carried food for three days, in the form of dried meat and rice, so were able to avoid going to villages, all of which were now inhabited by Burmese.

When their food was finished, Ras calculated that they would have to travel for a further six nights to get to the Arakan Yomas, including a crossing of the Irrawaddy River, where, once again, he could count on support from Karen villages. Had he been alone he would have avoided the danger of buying food from Burmese villages; as a result of his journeys in the Karenni States, he was as hard as nails and was sure that he could do without food for six days. But he had to consider Mura and, as the latter was a Kachin, he would be less likely to attract attention in the villages than would Ras.

They therefore worked out a plan to get enough food from one village to carry them through to the Irrawaddy. Ras remained outside under cover while Mura entered the village to buy food. They had agreed that if Mura came back carrying his hat, it would be safe for Ras to join him. However, if he returned with a party of villagers and his hat was on his head, Ras would know that Mura was a prisoner of the villagers. In that case Mura would suddenly fall to the ground to avoid being hit as Ras fired a burst at the party. In the ensuing confusion Mura would bolt away and join Ras. If Mura did not return to Ras but a party of villagers did so, then Ras would know that it was probably a trap and would be on his guard.

In the event the villagers must have become suspicious of Mura and had detained him in the village while some of them came out to persuade Ras to join him and to have a meal. He agreed reluctantly, motioned them to lead on, cocked his Tommy gun and took up a position at the rear of the party. He saw that the man immediately ahead of him was carrying a rifle on his shoulder, the muzzle of which pointed back at Ras, so he gradually dropped back until the man was well ahead of him.

Suddenly the Burman pulled the trigger of his rifle, luckily unaware that the force of the explosion would lift the muzzle, and the bullet whipped over Ras's head. At the same instant three or four men in the bushes ahead fired shotguns and, as he turned to run, Ras was caught by a charge of shot in his buttocks. He fired a whole magazine at them, killing the man with the rifle and probably some of the others. The survivors fled back to the village, leaving their dead and dying on the path.

Ras was certain that both of them would die if he tried to rescue Mura; he did not know how many men in the village were armed nor where they would be waiting to ambush him. Mura would have to use his wits and fend for himself, hoping to escape later, as they had agreed in such an eventuality.

Ras was now on his own; he guessed that, if he continued his journey north or west, every village would be on the look-out for him as they would assume that this was what he would do. Fortunately darkness had now fallen so he had the whole night in which to throw them off the scent and to find a safe hiding place for the following day. Accordingly he set off south, travelling as fast as he could throughout the night.

At dawn he found some thick cover and hid in it all day. But the hot weather had already begun in Burma and, on these plains, it was hotter than in the Karen hills, so he suffered from a raging thirst all day, not daring to come out into the open to look for water.

After dark he came out of hiding, found some water and drank his fill, and then marched in a westerly direction all night, taking cover before dawn. Unfortunately his hiding place was close to a small temple and, during the afternoon, he was spotted by a *pongyi* (Buddhist Monk) who made signs that he should come into the temple for a meal. Ras thought that he would be safe while he was inside the temple so ate the food. Several Burmans had come into the temple while he was eating and suddenly Ras noticed that, one by one, they were leaving. He had a feeling that treachery was afoot and he decided to leave without delay. Thanking the *pongyi* for the food, he cocked his Tommy gun and stepped warily out of the temple. As he did so he heard a shout and saw a crowd of Burmese, armed with *dahs* and crossbows, charging towards him. He started to run but one man caught up with him and began to grappled with him, trying to get his Tommy gun. Ras gave him a swift upper-cut, which floored him, and dashed into bushes which covered the area round the temple: He ran north as fast as he could, hotly pursued by the villagers, gradually gaining on them because they were frightened of his gun. At length, panting with thirst and utterly exhausted, he plunged into a dense thicket of prickly bushes, working his way into the centre of these, oblivious of the thorns which tore his flesh. The yelling mob swept past his lair and their cries faded as they searched further and further away from him. Fortunately, there were only two hours of daylight left and they did not get on his trail again.

At dusk he cautiously broke cover and set off south, reasoning that the Burmese would be certain that he would continue to flee north. But his thirst was now unendurable and he just had to find water. At last he came across some wells but found, to his dismay, that the water in all of them was salty. However, as his body needed salt after his sweating during his flight, he drank a little. Then he found another well; it had no rope or bucket but a bamboo pole, with cross-pieces lashed to it to make a ladder, went down into the well. It looked far from safe and he was now exhausted but was so desperate for water that he had to take a chance.

Gingerly he climbed down to the bottom of the well where, to his joy, he found fresh water. He drank until he could hold no more and then soaked his clothes and body in the water. It was such bliss that he could have stayed in the water all night but at last he climbed cautiously out of the well and searched for a hiding place during the last hour of darkness. He found a small bamboo hut which was surrounded by a close-knit fence of split bamboo. He sat in it for a couple of hours, alert in case the owners came there to work. When no one came he guessed that the hut was probably not used at this season of the year so lay down and cat-napped all day, deep sleep being too great a risk in the circumstances.

In the evening, having first drunk deeply at the well, he walked westwards all night. At daybreak he saw ahead of him a wide open plain, with no cover and few villages. In the distance a steep hill rose out of the plain and on the top of the hill was a *pagoda*. This was covered in gold leaf and shone in the sunlight like a beacon which made it appear nearer to him than it really was. As there was nowhere to hide, and the villages on the plain were sparse, he decided to push on in daylight to the hill. It was a risk, but he hoped that, if anyone did see him, his attire would mark him as a native. He was wearing thin, silky, green trousers, a shirt not tucked in, his turban and, as usual, he was barefooted. After a year of travelling in bare feet his soles were so thick and hard that they were impervious to stones and thorns.

He strode along all day under the scorching sun,
meeting no one, but the hill was further away than he had
estimated and, when night fell, he had only reached the
foot of it. Having been walking for 24 hours with no sleep,
he was exhausted and he decided to lie up for that night
and the next day and night to recoup his strength. The
base of the hill was thickly covered with bushes which
would give him concealment and shade the next day, so he
crawled into them and slept soundly.

He woke when the sun was up and got into a position
where he could observe the *pagoda*. He saw a few saffron-
robed monks moving about around it but no one else came
near it. He slept the night through and, at daybreak, much
refreshed but hungry, climbed the hill.

Outside the *pagoda* he was greeted by one of the monks
who, by a lucky chance, spoke a little English. He seemed
well-disposed and invited Ras into the *pagoda* to eat and
sleep. He said that the Burmese rarely came to this
isolated *pagoda* and that the Japanese had never visited it,
although he had met some soldiers on two occasions when
he had been away from the *pagoda*.

Ras was startled out of his sleep at about noon by the
sound of aircraft. He rushed out and stood with the monks
who were watching British or American aircraft bombing
Prome. As he watched, Ras suddenly had a good idea; the
matter of his identity under these dangerous circumstances
had been troubling his mind over the past weeks. If the
Japanese were to capture him and identify him as Pagani,
an escaped PoW, he would almost certainly be returned to
18 Km camp and shot. He decided that he would pretend
to be a lieutenant in the American Air Force who had
recently been shot down or had crashed. He chose to
impersonate an American rather than a British officer

because, as far as he knew, no Americans were fighting in Burma and, therefore, the Japanese would be unlikely to link an American officer with a British NCO who had escaped from the railway. He hoped that his 'rarity value' as an American in Burma would excite the curiosity of the Japanese and that they would then treat him properly as a PoW. He would take the Christian names of his baby son, Terry Ashton Melvyn, and use them as his Christian and surnames. Perhaps then he would be treated as a PoW and imprisoned in Burma instead of being sent back to the railway. It was a gamble, but he had nothing to lose as he was a dead man if identified as Pagani.

After the planes had gone the *pongyi* pointed out to Ras where Japanese troops were normally positioned, the Irrawaddy River, and, rising up tantalizingly the other side of the river, the Arakan Yomas. Ras was elated; the Irrawaddy was his last big hurdle and, after crossing it, he would again be among friendly Karens in the Arakan Yomas. He reckoned that he could reach the river in one night's walking.

He had felt safe among these *pongyis* although, remembering his previous experience in a temple, he had remained very alert and kept his Tommy gun with him at all times. On arrival he had counted their number and had checked on them at intervals during the day so that he would know if one had slipped away to inform the Japanese of his presence. But none had left the *pagoda*, the atmosphere had been relaxed and friendly and they genuinely appeared to like him or, at least, to feel sympathy for him.

However, now that his goal was in sight, he was anxious to continue his journey. He wrote out a chit which stated that these monks had been very helpful to him and gave it to the head *pongyi*. Ras told him to show it to the British when they returned, as they would surely do one day, but on no account to let the Japanese find it.

At dusk, bidding his kind hosts a final farewell, he descended the hill and made tracks for the Irrawaddy, refreshed, confident and full of hope. During his journey he heard Prome being subjected to another air raid. He reached the river without incident just before dawn and almost immediately found an excellent hiding place in a cave, the mouth of which was screened by thick bushes. Inside the cave there was a smell of big cats and Ras guessed that it had been occupied quite recently by a tiger or leopard. Having heard that these animals would probably be more afraid of him than he was of them, he felt confident that they would not enter the cave while he was inside, so settled down to sleep for an hour or two.

During the morning he carefully reconnoitred the river bank to see if there was a boat nearby but found none. He dared not go far from his cave in daylight in order to search further along the river so decided he would have to swim. The Irrawaddy here was about half a mile wide but this did not worry him as he was a strong swimmer.

Before starting he had one last task to carry out: Seagrim's long letter to Army HQ and his note promoting Ras to sergeant in the field he tore into small pieces and, together with his identity discs, buried them in the floor of the cave. They would have been incriminating documents for both Seagrim and himself if he was captured and the identity discs would be a death warrant for him. In any case he had no means of keeping the documents dry while he was swimming.

Now Sergeant Ras Pagani had disappeared from Burma and Lieutenant Terry Ashton Melvyn, a USAAF pilot, had taken his place. He felt a great sense of relief, although he realized that if he was later killed under this name no one would ever know what had happened to Pagani. It would probably be assumed that he had died alone in the jungle from disease or starvation.

After night had fallen Ras waited until the moon had risen. Then, slinging his Tommy gun over his shoulder, he waded into the river and started to swim across it. For about one hundred and fifty yards he made good progress but then he was seized by two fierce currents, one with a strong undertow, and was soon in difficulties. As he struggled to regain the surface the Tommy gun banged against his back and, together with the weight of his four spare magazines and two hand grenades, threatened to pull him below the surface and drown him. He knew that he had to jettison them; he needed the gun for his safety ashore but now it was going to kill him if he did not let it go. After doing this he came to the surface immediately and decided to float down the river rather than struggling against those terrible currents.

He hoped that a curve in the river would eventually deposit him on the far bank but, after floating down-river for about five miles, becoming increasingly exhausted, the currents drove him again onto the south bank. He had just crawled ashore and was lying, panting, on the mud, when two or three Burmans came towards him. He guessed that they were probably fishermen as they had a small boat with them. Rising to his feet, Ras made signs that he wished to be put across the river. They seemed to agree to this but he watched them like a hawk as he now had no weapon. He got into the boat and they pushed off. It appeared to him that they were delaying their departure from the beach unnecessarily and his suspicions became aroused.

Suddenly, a shout came from the river bank and, in the bright moonlight, he saw a crowd of about fifty Burmans, some armed with shotguns and others with *dahs*. They ordered the fishermen to return to the bank and Ras saw that all his struggles to remain free were now at an end, unless he later got a chance to escape his captors. It was a bitter moment; since leaving the Karenni States he had survived several narrow escapes from death or capture and now, at the very moment of success, he was once more a prisoner.

During the day the Arakan Yomas had seemed so close as he gazed across the river; there he would have found friends who would have guided him on his way north. But now they were as unattainable as if they had been on another planet.

As the boat came to shore the Burmans seized him. They tied a rope round him, over his arms (which he had the wit to keep away from his body so that the rope was loose), and then tied a short piece of rope to the first and prodded him ahead of them like a dog on a lead.

When they had gone a short distance he slipped his ropes and dashed off at full speed towards some bushes on the river bank. But his luck was out; he stubbed his toes in a crack in the dried mud and fell sprawling. He leapt to his feet; one of the Burmans was almost on top of him and Ras gave him a terrific upper-cut which knocked him senseless. He turned and darted off again. Suddenly he heard a loud explosion and felt a blow, followed by a terrible pain, in his side. His strength ebbed at once and he fell to the ground. In seconds the Burmans were on him, slashing him with their *dahs* and hitting him with clubs until he was barely conscious. Then they stopped and he was dimly aware that they were standing all round him.

He heard a dog snarling close to him, but when he slowly turned his head could not see it. Then he coughed and felt a searing pain in his right side. He coughed again and put a hand on his side to try and ease the pain. His hand came away wet and sticky and he saw dimly that he was holding a thick clot of blood large enough to fill his hand. The snarling continued and then he realized that it was not a dog but air bubbling through the hole in his side every time he breathed. His back and head also were agony where the Burmans had slashed him deeply with their *dahs*. (He carries terrible scars from these wounds today).

He was barely conscious but just alive enough to realize that this was the end for him; he was going to die; his promise to his wife and small son to return would not now be kept and they would never know what had become of him. He was going to die alone, without identity, in this distant land, among a hostile people.

He sank into a merciful coma.

CHAPTER TEN

Ante-room to Hell

How long he had lain on the river bank Ras did not know but, with the coming of dawn, he was dimly aware that the Burmese were carrying him. They laid him face downwards in the boat which they then poled upstream for a short distance to a Japanese post. While he lay in the boat a Japanese doctor stitched up the worst wound in his back, which was about a foot long and very deep, with an instrument which sewed up the wound automatically. By now all his wounds had stiffened and the feeling had come back into them so Ras suffered agonies while this was carried out with no anaesthetic.

These Japanese had apparently not been in action against·the Allies and treated him with some care and curiosity. They asked him from where he had come and he muttered that he was an American Flying Officer who had been shot down during the previous night's raid on Prome.

An ambulance arrived; Ras was lifted into it, taken to the main hospital in Prome and wheeled straight into the operating theatre.

The Japanese doctor here was a sadist who seemed to take a delight in causing Ras as much pain as possible. He took out all the stitches which the first doctor had put in and poked about in the wounds, oblivious to his victim's groans of pain. He spoke a little English so Ras asked him why he did not use anaesthetic and reduce the pain. The doctor replied smugly that wounded Japanese troops did not need anaesthetics and he certainly was not going to waste any on an American enemy. Ras, stirred to anger by this callous remark, replied that Americans could stand pain as well as any Japanese soldier.

After a time, to his surprise, he found that he had passed through a kind of pain barrier and agony itself became an anaesthetic. This was a mercy because the doctor continued to probe his wounds and four hours had passed before he stitched them up again. Ras, exhausted by his ordeal of the past eighteen hours, was put on a trolley, wheeled through a hospital ward and out into the grounds where he was dumped in a small round hut, similar to a summer house, under which a deep pit had been dug.

That night was the worst of his life. His wounds were so excruciatingly painful that eventually he decided it would be better to die than endure such agony any further. He said his prayers, placed a blood-stained towel over his face and tried to suffocate himself. Then, as his body struggled against his mind, he suddenly remembered his promise to his young wife that he would return to her. He threw the towel on the floor and, gritting his teeth, forced himself to bear the pain and to live out that long lonely night.

In the morning he was barely alive. The Japanese came and changed his dressings while he lay almost unconscious. This pattern of ghastly nights continued for several days after which he very slowly began to recover and felt that perhaps he would not die.

When he had recovered enough to speak, Japanese Intelligence officers came to interrogate him. He stuck to his story that he was an American pilot, Lieutenant Terry Ashton Melvyn, who had been shot down while on a night raid on Prome. He explained his clothes by saying that his uniform had caught fire when he had crashed and that a Burman had given him the clothes which he now wore. By now he almost believed his own story and, as it was tied to a raid known to the Japanese, it seemed to satisfy them. But he thought them rather inept in not noticing that he spoke without an American accent and that they did not grill him on what type of plane he had been flying during the raid.

Raids on Prome were frequent; at that time they were one of the few ways in which the embattled British forces in north Burma could strike back at the Japanese. One day a raid set most of Prome alight and the planes returned that night to complete the job. Ras was convinced he was going to be killed by a British bomb as they were falling all round the hospital and splinters frequently struck his frail hut. However, he felt a grim satisfaction at the fear shown by the Japanese. As soon as the air raid sirens sounded several of them came running to his hut and jumped down into the pit below it, hissing and chattering with fear. As he lay above them, Ras mocked them, telling them not to be afraid as he was protecting them with his body. Luckily they were too frightened of the bombs to avenge their loss of face on him.

As his health slowly improved he also learned how to get the better of the officers who came regularly to question him. He found that, by stalling the questions, saying that he was not bound to answer them under the

Geneva Convention, the Japanese, who were very conceited, would accidentally betray to him that they already knew the answers to the questions they were asking him. Eventually they would answer the questions themselves, exclaiming triumphantly, 'Is that not so?' He would then nod, as if reluctant to admit that they had outwitted him, and they would say, 'Ah so!' and go on to the next question. When they asked a question to which he realized they did not know the answer, and which might be detrimental to him if he gave one, he would say that his wounds were so painful that he could not think clearly or remember past events, and he would emphasize this by pretending to faint. Then they would leave him alone until another day.

After about six weeks in this hut his wounds had healed to some extent; he had enjoyed rest and adequate food and was just able to walk, although he was still very weak, especially in his back muscles.

Then, early one morning, two Japanese soldiers came to collect him. They took him to the railway station and escorted him to Rangoon. As the train clanked slowly through the countryside Ras, now confident in his new identity and with no fear of being returned to 18 Km camp, assumed that he was being taken to a PoW camp in Rangoon where he would join other Allied prisoners.

But he was in for a very nasty shock.

On arrival at Rangoon station his escort took him to the New Law Courts, where they handed him over. Ras realized almost at once that he was now in the hands of the dreaded *Kempeitai*; he knew that few of their prisoners lived long enough to be released, that many were tortured to death or executed, and that all suffered terrible hardships and ill-health as a result of brutal treatment.

He was pushed into a cell with five other men, all natives, and he later learned that he was the only military prisoner in these cells. The cell was about ten by eight feet; three men had to squat on each side of it and they were not allowed to move except to go to the latrine bucket which stood in one corner. The prisoners were not allowed to speak to each other and Japanese sentries patrolled the passage in front of the cells to ensure that they did not do so. The lights were on all day and night.

The front of the cell, looking on to the passage, consisted of stout wooden bars, three inches by one inch thick, which ran from floor to ceiling. Entry to the cell was by a small trap door about two feet square, situated at ground level and, alongside this, was a gap in the bars at floor level, about six inches square, through which small bowls of food were shoved each morning and evening. The food consisted of a small quantity of rice over which had been poured a watery stew of vegetables or shrimps.

It was a revolting place, dirty and stinking of excrement and Ras's spirits fell like a stone. On arrival he had been ordered to occupy a space next to the bars and this proved to be a minor blessing; not only did he get a breath of what little fresh air there was in the passage but, every evening, a Japanese soldier came round with a flit gun which he sprayed through the bars of each cell. Within days Ras was, like his companions, covered with lice and he begged the Japanese to spray his head and crotch every evening, a request which so amused the soldier that he granted it. It served to keep the lice at bay to some extent.

The first morning gave him a foretaste of the treatment he could expect. Two guards came to his cell and dragged out one of the inmates whom they then beat and kicked along the passage to the interrogation rooms. For the next two hours they heard thuds as the man was beaten unmercifully, the shouts of the Japanese mingling with the screams of their victim. At last the guards dragged him back, half-conscious, and kicked him into the cell. His face was black and blue, his nose streaming with blood and his fingers and toes very swollen. One of the inmates tried to help the man to sit up but a sentry in the passage screamed at him and threatened him with similar treatment. The unfortunate man just lay on the floor of the cell until he came to his senses again. Each day a prisoner was taken out and those remaining had to endure his screams as the Japanese tortured him.

After a few days they came for Ras. As he crawled on all fours out through the trap door they kicked him and beat him about the head and shoulders with sticks. He staggered to his feet and had to run to the end of the passage, pursued by the Japanese who slashed at his buttocks and barely-healed back. This was just to soften him up for what was to follow.

There were three interrogation rooms; the first was bare except for two chairs on which sat two Japanese soldiers with canes. Ras was made to kneel between them. One, obviously *Kempeitai*, would question him in bad English. Every time he answered they would scream and rave at him, slashing him with their canes. This continued for about half an hour. Then they dragged him to the next room, which was exactly the same except that one of the men was an officer. Again he had to kneel between them; the officer drew his sword and kept beating him with the flat of it after each question. Then he would put his empty pistol to Ras's head and pull the trigger and, finally, he would practise sword-play, bringing the sharp edge of the sword swiftly down onto Ras's neck, checking it only at the moment it touched his skin. (Ras learned later that this unnerving performance had finished several natives who had literally died of fright at this stage, although several were beheaded either intentionally or because the officer had misjudged his swing.) These sadists deliberately slashed and prodded his newly-healed and very tender wounds so that he often passed out with the pain.

But the worst room was the third one, in which he often felt that he would lose his reason. It was like a wash-house, with a concrete floor and a drain in one corner. He would be made to lie on his back on the floor, his arms and legs tied to rings let into the concrete. These were so positioned that his head was directly below a slow-dripping tap; every few seconds it loosed a drop which hit him between the eyes. At first it caused him no trouble but gradually the pain built up until he felt as if each drop was a cannon-ball landing on his forehead. They would leave him for about half an hour until he had reached this state and then come in and start questioning him again. Sometimes they would put slivers of bamboo under his finger and toenails, up his nose and in his private parts, and would then set them alight. After that he would be dragged half-conscious back to his cell, to await the next session of torture, which might take place later that day.

How he survived these tortures he does not know; over forty years later he is still reluctant to talk of them because thought of them brings back the nightmare of those days. There were times when he felt that he could stand it no longer and would prefer to die by his own hand. This treatment would kill him in any case if it went on much longer and he was resigned to the likelihood that he would be executed in due course. Then the picture of his wife and baby son would come back to his mind; he had promised them he would return and this strengthened his resolve to hold out against his sadistic torturers. But there was always the fear that, when they had become tired of playing with him, they would just take him out and execute him. He had witnessed this so often; when the cells were full and new victims arrived, the Japanese would drag out those who had been there longest and kill them.

In this hellish place he could find only two crumbs of comfort. First, after a time incessant exposure to pain mercifully numbed his tortured body so that pain was actually reduced; second, he had long since realized that his interrogators were not interested in getting the truth from him. Their questions, and the tortures which followed, were intended to humiliate him and break him as a human being. Consequently, he felt certain that they would never question his new identity.

But how much longer he could endure these brutalities he did not know. After about six weeks of living in this nightmare he was very weak and getting weaker, his mind often wandering as he became semi-conscious after these sessions of torture. He realized that there might come a time when his body would just give up and he would die.

One morning they came for him as usual and he steeled himself to face another bout of torture. But, to his surprise, they took him outside and put him into a lorry. Convinced that he was being taken to a place of execution he said some prayers. This was the end of the road for him, he thought bitterly; he would have been better off if the Burmese had killed him by the Irrawaddy and saved him all this suffering.

They stopped outside Rangoon jail; the *Kempeitai* escort kicked him out of the lorry, handed him over to Japanese guards at the jail and drove off.

Ras was taken before an interpreter who told him that he would be put in solitary confinement. The guards escorted him to an upper floor, pushed him into a cell and slammed the door.

He sank onto the plank bed and eased his bruised body. A new chapter was beginning; whatever it brought for him could not be worse than life in the *Kempeitai* prison. Comforted by this thought he fell asleep.

CHAPTER ELEVEN

Rangoon Jail

For a moment, after he had woken, he did not know where he was. Then the realization that he was out of the hands of the *Kempeitai* came back to his mind and he suddenly felt very cheerful. He looked around his cell; it was about eight feet by four and, as it was on an upper landing, he had a view over a courtyard where he could see Europeans, presumably prisoners of war. A plank bed and wooden pillow were the only furniture apart from an old ammunition box which served as a latrine bucket.

He found it a joy to be alone again; living cheek by jowl with natives in the *Kempeitai* cell had seemed more lonely as they were so alien to him. He was still very weak but saw that, as he could lie on the bed all day and rest, his health would improve rapidly.

Every morning he, and the inmates of cells on the landing, were paraded for *tenko*. They had to carry out their latrine buckets and empty them. But his back muscles were still so weak he could carry the heavy ammunition box only a few paces before having to set it down and rest. At first the guards beat him up when he did this but, when it at last dawned on them that he really was unable to carry the box, they ordered one of the natives to carry it for him.

Interrogations and beatings were an almost daily occurrence but were not as severe as those meted out by the *Kempeitai*, nor were there any torture sessions. On one occasion Ras asked his interrogator, who spoke passable English, what was the object of this continual ill-treatment as they already knew everything about him. He got the reply that it was necessary in order 'to teach him discipline the Japanese way'.

Then, suddenly, in the illogical manner that became so familiar to those who had to live under the Japanese yoke, they lost interest in him, utterly and completely, and from that time onwards the interrogators left him alone.

Only one Japanese continued to visit him and to question him in a rather disinterested way. He was a bit of a simpleton; his understanding of English was poor and Ras was amazed to learn that he was the official inter-preter for the prisoner of war camp. To each of Ras's answers he exclaimed the usual 'Ah so!' So Ras rudely christened him 'Arse-hole' and derived a childish satis-faction from this obscene nickname.

Simple though the man appeared, one day he gave Ras a terrible shock. The reason for his rather aimless visits became apparent when he asked Ras if he would teach him English. Keeping up his deception about his true identity, Ras jokingly replied that he could only teach him American. The interpreter looked slyly at him for a moment and then said, 'You no American officer, you English,' and he pointed to the tattoos on Ras's arms and chest, one of which was in French.

For a second Ras felt as if he had been kicked in the

stomach and his blood ran cold. This apparently stupid little runt was questioning his identity, the first Japanese to do so. Ras saw immediately that he must humour the man or he might turn nasty and return him to the *Kempeitai* for further questioning about his real name. He knew that he would not survive another stretch of their treatment and, once they had wrung from him his real name, his fate would be sealed and all his sufferings would have been in vain.

It was a moment fraught with danger; keeping his wits about him, Ras replied, as calmly as he was able, that he *had* been English by birth but had taken American nationality several years ago.

This reply satisfied the man and Ras heaved an inward sigh of relief. But he hoped that the interpreter would not discuss his suspicions with his comrades, some of whom were more mentally alert than he was and might start asking dangerous questions.

Ras asked the interpreter what it would be worth to him if he agreed to teach him English. When the man said that he would bring him extra food, sweet cakes and cigarettes, Ras agreed and every afternoon thereafter the interpreter would collect him and take him to his office. While Ras ate the food and smoked the cigarettes, he did his best to improve the man's English, reflecting that it could only do good if it helped to reduce misunderstandings between the Japanese and prisoners in the jail.

One of the first things Ras demanded of his pupil was a mirror so that he could shave. This the interpreter produced, but, witless creature that he was, did not apparently notice that Ras continued to wear his beard. Next morning, after *tenko* was over, Ras, who had been trained as a signaller in India where heliographs were in common use before the war, set to work to exchange messages with those men he could see in the compound. They quickly responded and he learned many items of interest including the information that the senior British officer was a brigadier.

This signalling in the mornings and the English lessons he was giving to 'Arse-hole' in the afternoons, filled his time and raised his spirits. The extra food supplied by the interpreter and plenty of rest were rapidly restoring him to health and life was good compared with the earlier weeks.

Before long he was to have a very pleasant surprise. The Japanese, once they had locked the cells every evening, never came near them again until the morning *tenko*. One of the natives in another cell had made a skeleton key and it was his custom to open all the cell doors at night so that the inmates could gather in one cell and chat together during the hours of darkness. One evening after dark Ras was astonished to see his cell door slowly opening and then, standing in the doorway grinning all over his face, his faithful Mura. He had brought a plate of food which the other occupants of the cells had saved from their evening meal. Ras was immensely touched by this kind gesture of the natives towards him, many of whom, he discovered, were Karens. For the next two months Mura came to see him every night, bringing titbits from the cells below, and the Japanese never detected these 'dormitory parties'.

At their first meeting Ras explained to Mura his reasons for changing his identity and impressed on him that he must *never* admit to the Japanese that he had previously known Ras nor that Ras had fought in the Karen Levies.

Sometimes Mura brought others with him and they would sit, quietly laughing and talking, most of the night.

These gatherings gave his morale a tremendous boost and he also welcomed the extra food. But he felt both pride and sadness in Mura's devotion to him. What had he ever done for Mura except to take him into dangerous situations which had landed him at last in the *Kempeitai* torture chambers? Mura could have stayed in the Karenni States in relative safety, biding his time until the war was over or a new resistance force was formed. But he had chosen to share the risks of an Englishman, who stuck out like a sore thumb among the natives and whose chances of evading eventual capture were slight. Ras was much moved by Mura's faithful service to him.

At the end of two months Mura slipped in one night and said that he was being released the next day. Apparently the Japanese were satisfied that their vile treatment of Mura had brainwashed him sufficiently and that now he was a fit person to release into their 'co-prosperity sphere' and would, in future, co-operate with the Japanese.

Mura had said nothing to dispel their illusions but told Ras that he would slowly make his way back to the Karenni States and rejoin the resistance movement.

Ras felt sad at the prospect of losing his company but was delighted that he was to be released and only wished he could go with him. He never saw Mura again.

He remained in solitary confinement for another three or four months and was then sent to join the other prisoners of war in the compound. By now his wounds had healed and he felt fit. He was put into a section of the compound which was under the command of an Indian Army major. Ras felt that he ought to confide in his new commanding officer his real name and the reason he had changed his identity. But, to his astonishment, the major said that, as a sergeant, he could not live among the officers, but must move in with the British Other Ranks. Apparently the major did not mind him living under a false name or as a member of the American Air Force but he objected to Ras masquerading as an officer. Ras explained patiently that as his 'cover' was that he had been shot down while piloting a bomber, and he had assumed that a pilot would have been an officer, he had had to pretend to be an officer to make his story convincing to the Japanese. Feeling a rising anger, he coldly pointed out to the major that, if the Japanese suddenly found that they were short of an American officer but had an extra British sergeant, they would start asking awkward questions. He would then be handed back to the *Kempeitai* and eventually executed, and the major would also undoubtedly incur their displeasure for having made this switch of ranks without informing the Japanese of the reason for it. Was he prepared to go now and tell the Japanese of Ras's true identity and thereby sign the latter's death warrant?

The major blustered; he said that of course he would not tell the Japanese but he was adamant that Ras could not continue to live with the British officers. He was posing as an American officer, so he could go and live with the ten Americans in their section, if they would have him. But, he added, on no account was he to attempt any further escape because the Japanese would then take reprisals against himself and perhaps other prisoners.*

Ras was flabbergasted by the major's attitude and this distasteful episode continued to rankle with him. There-

---

* The major was on firmer ground here. Earlier on the Japanese had executed twenty prisoners in reprisal for an escape by one man from Rangoon jail. See *MI9* Escape and Evasion 1939–45, by M. R. D. Foot and J. M. Langley, Bodley Head, London, 1979.

after he always had an uneasy feeling that the major who, by reason of his position of authority in the compound, was in close and even friendly daily contact with the Japanese, might one day betray him. If he did, and the suspicions of 'Arse-hole' were added, Ras would die for certain. He compared the major's treatment of him bitterly with the easy relationship he had enjoyed with Seagrim.

He went to see the senior American officer, Major Lutz. The American listened in silence to his story and then clapped him on the shoulder and told him to 'move in with his boys', adding that he did not like the British major either. Ras joined the Americans, who gave him a great welcome and he made friends with all of them, especially with a Lieutenant Humphries who took Ras under his wing. Humphries, like Ras, never missed an opportunity of 'taking the mickey' out of the Japanese.

Soon after this episode an American Colonel joined them; he told Humphries that he had been promoted to the rank of captain, a privilege not enjoyed by British prisoners, who remained throughout their captivity in the rank which they had held when captured.

The arrival of this colonel caused quite a stir; the Japanese appointed him senior officer in the compound, although there were only about ten Americans in the jail. The Indian Army major refused to accept this and open hostility developed between the two officers. Eventually wiser heads came to the rescue and it was agreed that the major would command all the British and Australian prisoners while the Colonel would be answerable to the Japanese for the whole compound. The Japanese, of course, knew nothing of this petty strife so the system worked quite well.

Much has been written about life in Japanese prison camps and the facts are well known to most readers. As the aim of this book is to chronicle Ras Pagani's escapes and his operations under Seagrim with the Karen resistance movement, his life as a PoW for the next eighteen months is irrelevant and a repetition of widely known accounts. Suffice it to say that he experienced the same life as has been so often recounted by others; the boredom, the smuggling of extra food in from the camp gardens (in which the American Colonel had at last obtained permission for the officers to work each day), the dirt and disease, the stoic heroism of many and the frequent deaths and burials.*

There was, however, one important difference between life in Rangoon jail and life in the more permanent camps in Singapore and Siam – the total lack of any information from outside concerning the progress of the war.

They had no clandestine radio receivers such as most camps enjoyed, few outside working parties, so few contacts with the local population (apart from Indians, most were, in any case, hostile to them); the guards were all Japanese so there was no chance of information from dissident Korean guards, as occurred in other camps, and they were surrounded by a solid stone wall fifteen feet high so could not even see out of the compound. Furthermore, all recently captured prisoners were kept separate from them, presumably to prevent news of the war spreading through the jail. They were thus as isolated from the outside world as if they had been imprisoned on an island in the middle of the Indian Ocean.

They had, however, noted the increasing number of

---

* Several references to Pagani, under the pseudonym 'Pinky', occur in *The Rats of Rangoon* by Lionel Hudson, Leo Cooper, 1987.

air-raids by Allied planes and hoped that this pointed to a turning of the tide against the Japanese. But American advances in the Pacific, 14th Army's victorious advance south through Burma, Russian victories over the Germans and the invasion of Europe by the Allies, were totally unknown to them, living as they did in this limbo.

But, in spite of his horrifying experiences at the hands of the *Kempeitai*, the veto on escaping placed on him by the Indian Army major and the seeming impossibility of getting out of the jail, Ras never gave up hope of making another escape if the opportunity were to arise. He kept himself fit and awaited his chance; it was to come in less than a year, although not quite in the manner he had imagined it.

Ras often thought of Seagrim although he knew nothing, of course, of what had happened to him after he had hurriedly left Pyagawpu on 25 February, 1943. One day, by a curious sequence of events, he was to find out something about Seagrim, that he was in Japanese hands and actually in the jail. By the time he knew this it was too late to establish contact and Seagrim had been executed. It came about in the following manner.

Just inside the entrance to the jail the Japanese guardroom lay to the left and a line of cells, on two levels, were on the right. Originally they had been cells to hold first offenders but it was generally assumed that they now held natives of Rangoon who had committed petty crimes. Adjacent to the cells was a compound which was not in use and here sacks of rice were stored. Ras was sometimes put on a working party to carry sacks of rice from the compound to the camp cookhouse. Although they walked past these cells, they had never seen any of the inmates.

One day someone told Ras that one of the cells was

occupied by a British officer but he gave it little thought. Then, at the beginning of September, he was on the same working party and noticed a truck standing outside the cells. When he returned with another load the truck was just moving out of the gate, loaded with natives and Japanese guards. One of the natives was a tall bearded man whom he took to be an Indian; the man waved to him and Ras waved back but was puzzled by the incident as he knew no one in that part of the jail, let alone an Indian.

It nagged at his mind for some days and then, suddenly, it dawned on him that it had been Seagrim who had waved to him. But he did not know until much later that the truck was carrying Seagrim and several Karens, including Ras's old friend Ah Din, to their execution at the Kemmendine Cemetery. The memory of this last sight of his comrades in arms has haunted him all his life.

CHAPTER TWELVE

Operation 'Character': The Karens Rise Up

While Ras Pagani was serving out his last few weeks of captivity in Rangoon jail – quite unaware that the end was nearer than he would have dreamed in his most optimistic moments – great matters were afoot in the Karen hills.

The departure of Ras in the spring of 1943, the deaths of Major Nimmo and Captain McCrindle in February, 1944, Seagrim's voluntary surrender in mid-March the same year and the arrest of most of the Levy commanders and many Karen elders, had broken the Karen resistance movement. For several months thereafter persecution of the remaining Karens continued until they had become completely cowed. Then, some of those arrested but against whom no charges had been proved, were allowed to return to their homes, shaken and filled with a sense of defeat, and the Japanese took some of the pressure off the Karenni States. Few had the courage or inclination to rebuild a resistance force and most Karens, after their traumatic experiences at the hands of the Japanese, decided to lie low and to resume their normal lives, in the hope that the Japanese would leave them in peace.

The Allies also decided that the Karens were too far away to help effectively, so should not be encouraged to rise up again until our forces had fought their way further south and were in a position to give close and massive support to the Karens.

In northern Burma by the end of June, 1944 the Japanese 15th Army had virtually been destroyed in its fanatical attempts to capture Kohima and Imphal. They were betrayed by their commanders' arrogant assumption that, as in the past, they would be victorious and would capture supplies at these places, so they had paid insufficient attention to their own supply line which ran for miles through wild and terrible country. At last, starving, riddled with disease, short even of ammunition and deluged by the monsoon, this broken Army staggered back to the Chindwin River, leaving thousands to die by the wayside.

Allied forces regrouped and, after the monsoon, began to advance south rapidly. By March, 1945, they had crossed the Irrawaddy River and had captured the key defensive positions of Mandalay and Meiktila, in the process of which they destroyed many more Japanese.

General Slim, commanding 14th Army, now had to make a crucial decision; should he consolidate his gains in the north, sit out the monsoon – which would play such havoc with his ever-lengthening supply lines – and then continue the attack when the dry weather came, with all the advantages he had of superiority in tanks, artillery and aircraft, or should he make a lightning dash for Rangoon, while he had the enemy on the run, and thereby capture a port which would solve all his supply problems? He had only two months left before the arrival of the monsoon and was still three hundred miles from Rangoon by routes east of the Irrawaddy River; over four hundred miles if he were to go via Yenangyaung and Prome to the west.

To make a dash for Rangoon would be a great gamble, but the fruits of success would be tremendous. But could the Japanese delay him at any stage so that the monsoon arrived before he reached Rangoon, bringing his advance to a halt in a sea of mud and reducing his supplies to a trickle? He had only too vividly before him the disaster which had recently overtaken the Japanese when they had overstretched their supply line and then been caught by the monsoon; he had no wish to assume their mantle when everything was in his favour. He weighed in the balance the damage to the morale of 14th Army if he were to order it to stop its advance before the monsoon; he knew, too, that this would give the shattered Japanese forces a chance to rest, regroup and prepare strong defensive positions from which they could later inflict heavy casualties on 14th Army. This would be an unacceptable situation so he decided to go hell for leather for Rangoon using both routes.

This vital decision having been made, he had to consider where the Japanese would make every effort to delay his advance. There were two towns where he felt certain they would fight to the death to bring his advance to a halt – Toungoo, just west of the northern part of the Karenni States and a vital bottle-neck to Japanese forces trying to withdraw to Moulmein or into Siam, and Pegu, a rail centre about fifty miles north-east of Rangoon. The former posed the greater threat because there were three strong Japanese divisions in the Shan States; it was *vital* that these should be prevented from withdrawing south to Toungoo to make a formidable base there. Slim was going to need all the help he could get to delay these divisions and who could do it better than the Karens, if properly armed and well led?

Irregular forces, raised and armed by Force 136, had already been established with success in the hill states further north, among the Kachin and Chin races, and now it was time to enlist and arm the Karens to carry out this vital delaying operation north of Toungoo, and also to prevent the Japanese from withdrawing through the Karenni States to Siam where they would be able to rest, regroup and fight again.

Operation 'Character' was set up and put into action. It was organized to operate in four areas: *Walrus* (Lt.-Col. J. C. Tulloch) in the jungles north of the Mawchi road, *Otter* (Lt.-Col. E. H. Peacock) to cover both flanks of the Mawchi road from Bawlake in the eastern hills to the foothills near Toungoo in the west, *Hyena* (Major R. G. Turrall and, later, Lt.-Col. H. W. Howell) to occupy the area around Pyagawpu, Seagrim's old stamping ground, and *Mongoose* (Lt.-Col. R. A. Critchley MC) to operate in the Papun – Shwegyin – Bilin triangle where Ras Pagani had fought under Seagrim's orders in 1943.

The first to arrive was Major Turrall who dropped at Pyagawpu on 20 February, 1945. He found the Karens understandably nervous and unenthusiastic about joining him. However, a landing on 23 and 24 February by two Dakota loads of British, Burmese and Karen troops of *Otter* put heart into the Karens who rushed to enlist. Soon 600 had joined and Peacock, with no time to lose, moved north to his area of operations, into which he had not dropped as intended because many lights seen at the time had led him to suspect that Japanese troops were camped there. One of Peacock's officers was a brother of Major Nimmo who, as already related, had been killed in that area.

Howell also dropped into Pyagawpu with *Hyena* and set up shop there and, in March, Tulloch parachuted in with *Walrus* to the north of the Mawchi road, while Critchley, with *Mongoose*, took over in the south.

Altogether over one hundred British officers and NCOs, and about two hundred Karens and Burmese, flew in with 'Character' and, before long, had enlisted and armed twelve thousand Karens. The latter were encouraged to employ the tactics taught them by Seagrim – to ambush, hit hard and get out fast, *never* confronting the Japanese from static defensive positions – but now they had modern weapons in place of the old Italian rifles and faulty ammunition which they had had in Seagrim's day.

In mid-April the Japanese 15th Division began to move south from the Shan States towards Toungoo and it was estimated that they would arrive at about the same time as 14th Army's spearhead *unless* they could be delayed en route. This was achieved brilliantly by Peacock and Tulloch who harassed them to such an extent that the Division was delayed a whole week and arrived at Toungoo to find the town already firmly held by 14th Army.

Japanese troops in west and central Burma were also retreating south-east in a desperate attempt to reach Siam, and the two other divisions in the Shan States also moved south, but all their routes to safety passed through the Karenni States and, from May onwards, these were blocked by the Karens armed by 'Character'. Continuous fighting took place in the hills throughout the summer and at least 12,000 Japanese were killed directly by Karens and many more by Force 136 and Karen leaders who directed air strikes against them. Karen casualties were minimal; for example, *Otter* killed over 3,000 Japanese for the loss of only thirty-four Karens and *Hyena* over 5,000 for a similar loss. Only about half-a-dozen British were killed. Fighting continued in the hills after the Japanese surrender because some Japanese did not know – or could not believe – that the war was over, but eventually these stragglers were rounded up.

Peacock reported that the spirit of the Karens, once they had regained their confidence in their fighting abilities, was a tribute to Seagrim's work in earlier years when he had given them leadership and faith to fight for their race. They had now taken their revenge for the years of suffering under the Japanese and had upheld the honour of their 'father', Hugh Seagrim, who had given his life in a vain attempt to save them from persecution.

It is sad to have to relate that their victory over the hated Japanese was only the beginning of a long and bloody struggle against their traditional enemy, the Burmese, and although for a time they achieved a measure of peace and independence, at the time of writing they are again under threat and refugees are pouring into Thailand. Their loyalty to the British will never be forgotten by those who fought alongside them, although, once Burma had gained independence, we were powerless to help them in their struggle.

CHAPTER THIRTEEN

The Dangerous Road to Freedom

Soon after mid-April, 1945, the Japanese demanded a Roll of all men who were fit to march. Rumours of a move to a new camp flashed round the compound for several days and Ras was determined to get into the 'fit' party so that he could make yet another escape and return to the Karenni States.

Within a few days a party of about 500 officers and men had been pronounced fit to march, a damning indictment of Japanese treatment of prisoners of war because over 1000 were unfit to march – even by Japanese standards – and remained in the jail.

On 25 April this party marched out and headed north, Ras Pagani among them. The camp commandant, Captain Sumida, was in charge and took with him Matsuda, the stupid but sly interpreter whom Ras had nicknamed 'Arse-hole' during his time in solitary confinement. The prisoners soon found that this was going to be no easy stroll but rather a forced march from dawn to dusk each day. Many, who had considered themselves fit, suffered from their years of close confinement in the jail, where exercise was almost impossible, and fell behind the column where they were subjected to brutal beatings by the Japanese guards. Some were able to go no further and occasionally shots were heard as the Japanese killed these stragglers. Ras tried to drag along a dark-haired soldier who was becoming exhausted but, at last, the man could go no further and sank to the ground. A guard approached, shot the soldier through the head, and then screamed at Ras to get moving, threatening him with his rifle. Ras needed no further bidding as he saw that the guard was working himself up into a fury which was so characteristic of the Japanese guards before they went berserk.

After covering about fifteen miles they stopped in a valley between two small hills. Rice and raw onions were issued and they were told to cook their meals individually as there were no cooking pots. Scores of small fires were lit to cook the meals and these must have given away their position because, at dawn, a flight of Hurricanes swooped on them and straffed them with cannon-fire. Fortunately there were no casualties but it delayed their start and the Japanese began to get hysterical and lashed out at all and sundry. The prisoners were now made to leave the road and move across country, much of it dry *padi* fields of stubble which played havoc with the bare feet of those who had not, like Ras, hardened their feet over their years of captivity.

That day's march was gruelling. It was dark before they stopped, still out in open fields where they felt very vulnerable to attack by aircraft. Ras felt that there was no future in being killed by our own aircraft at this stage of the war and suggested to Major Lutz and Captain Humphries that they should make a break for it now and get away to the Karen hills where they would be safe. His companions advised waiting until they were nearer to the Sittang River towards which Ras knew they were now heading.

At dawn the Hurricanes attacked them again but without causing any casualties. No one could understand why the pilots of these fighters could not *see* that they were an unarmed straggling mob of prisoners and not Japanese troops.*

Throughout the day they were driven on by the guards for about thirty miles before collapsing, exhausted, into a small copse where they slept like the dead. During the night Ras and the Americans were lying quite close to Brigadier Hobson, the Senior British Officer. Just after waking in the morning Ras heard the Brigadier exclaim: 'By God! The bastards have deserted us!' Ras sat up and looked round the copse; there was not a sign of the guards. The Brigadier called them all together, told them that the Japanese had left, and advised them to stay put in the copse until more was known about the situation.

Now it was light and aircraft began to roam the skies. Some prisoners had red blankets so the Brigadier told the owners to lay them on the ground outside the copse, in the form of a red cross. Meanwhile Ras, a trained signaller, took the mirror which 'Arse-hole' had given him when he had been in solitary confinement and tried to attract the attention of passing aircraft and to send them a message.

* The reason was simple: those captured in the early stages of the Burma campaign had been wearing khaki-drill uniform, similar in colour to the Japanese uniform. Furthermore, prior to the march out of the jail, those whose uniforms had long since disintegrated were issued with cast-off Japanese uniforms. Jungle green uniforms had been universally worn by 14th Army for about two years, so pilots attacked any bodies of men wearing khaki, never dreaming that they might be allied PoWs. Similar errors also occurred in Europe.

Alas, neither his mirror nor the red blankets were to bring them salvation; Hurricanes, prowling the skies and hungry for targets, shot up the copse. Brigadier Hobson was killed and it was a miracle that there were not heavy casualties among the other prisoners.

Ras decided that it was time to go and tried again to persuade Lutz and Humphries to come with him. While they were talking, someone pointed out aircraft dropping supplies only a few miles away and then they heard artillery fire. This could only mean that our forces were drawing closer to them. Volunteers were called for to try and contact our forces. Finally, Lutz was selected to go as he still had what passed for uniform. As he was short and tubby he declined to go in disguise for fear that he might be mistaken for a Japanese or Burman by our side and shot, nor did he wish to risk being shot as a spy by any Japanese he might encounter. Meanwhile the others were ordered to remain in the copse, hoping that the Hurricanes would not return.

It was a hazardous undertaking; Lutz was well aware that Japanese troops were probably between him and units of 14th Army. If he were to run into them they would undoubtedly kill him. In addition there was the danger that, moving in the open in daylight, he might become a target for artillery or Hurricanes.

When he had gone the others concealed themselves in the copse and waited, tense with fear and hope, for several hours. It was afternoon when they saw a convoy of lorries approaching from the north; anxiety mounted; were the lorries Japanese or from 14th Army? At last the convoy drew up outside the copse; peering out cautiously from the trees the prisoners saw, with relief, that the markings on the trucks were definitely not Japanese. They went mad with joy and surged out to meet Lutz who had guided the convoy to them.

It was a glorious moment – one never to be forgotten for the rest of their lives; they were *free* at last and the Japanese nightmare had come to an end. Their joy was muted by sadness at the last-minute death of Brigadier Hobson, whom everyone liked and respected, but they had seen so much death during the past three years that even this tragedy could not dim their joy at their release. They had survived the years of misery and uncertainty – there was little room for anything else in their minds at that moment.

Nothing so wonderful would ever happen to them again.

The release of the sick PoWs from Rangoon jail was also attended by dangers, the degree of which they were not, perhaps mercifully, fully aware at the time.

Lieutenant-General Kimura, whose HQ (Burma Area Army), was in the city, and who had been ordered earlier to hold Rangoon to the last man and the last round – an order which might well have resulted in the deaths of all PoWs in the jail – decided that his orders were 'unrealistic' in view of the swift advance of British and Indian forces towards Pegu and the Sittang River. He therefore set in motion the evacuation of his HQ eastwards and himself flew to the safety of Moulmein. Whether by intention or by error, he did not inform Major-General Matsui, whom he had previously ordered to collect together a scratch force to defend Rangoon to the death and to destroy all port installations, that he was leaving.

When Matsui heard that Kimura had fled he could not, at first, believe it but when he visited the HQ buildings and found them empty and already being looted by the Burmese, he was consumed with rage against his superior officer. After he had calmed down he decided to deal first with the PoWs in the jail. He had already sent off the fit men, Pagani among them, towards the east with a view to moving them to Moulmein and on to Thailand. He now sent a secret message to Captain Sumida, the jail commandant, who was leading the marching PoWs, giving him discretion to release the prisoners if circumstances should dictate that this was the only thing to do. On 29 April he sent a message to the jail to say that food and medicines had been left in the jail for them and that they could either await rescue by their approaching forces or could leave if they so wished. A copy of this order was nailed on the main gate of the jail. Matsui then set out with his motley force to join the fighting around Pegu. Once more, from the safe haven of Moulmein, Kimura ordered him to return to Rangoon and to carry out his original orders. But, by this time, it was too late to retreat to Rangoon; Pegu was being attacked by strong armoured forces and Matsui, who had already lost part of his force in the Pegu battle, including some of his commanders, knew that there was no hope of reaching Rangoon. He therefore gathered in the remnants of his force and slipped away east into the Pegu Yomas, leaving Rangoon undefended.

The prisoners stayed in the jail; it seemed the sensible thing to do as they could not have moved out the seriously sick and it was unthinkable that these should be abandoned in the jail at this late stage in the war. Furthermore, Rangoon city was in chaos; bands of Burmese criminals and *dacoits*, many of them armed, roamed the city, looting and killing. The prisoners had seen many of our aircraft flying over the city during those few days so decided to send them a message. They painted in large letters on the jail roof – 'JAPS GONE' – and added, for good measure, – 'EXTRACT DIGIT'. The prisoners were not to know that Rangoon was about to be invaded from the sea but their message reached the invasion force commander. It was discussed and while it was thought just possible that the first part of the message might be a cunning Japanese trap, it was inconceivable that they would have thought of the second part of the message. However, it was decided that the invasion would go ahead as planned on the assumption that the Japanese might still be defending some areas of the city unknown to those in the jail. Early on 1 May the assault began with a parachute drop of troops on Elephant Point, which controlled the channel into Rangoon, and with saturation bombing on intended beach-heads.

One officer at least had no doubts about the validity of the message which he had seen as he had flown over Rangoon the previous day. Wing Commander A. E. Saunders, commanding 110 Squadron R.A.F. (Mosquitoes), flew low over Mingaladon airfield and, finding it deserted, came in to land. The runway had been so badly cratered by R.A.F. bombing that he was lucky to get down in one piece. His aircraft burst a tyre on landing so there was no question of it taking off again.

Undaunted, he and his navigator, Flight Lieutenant Fletcher, set out on foot for the jail where they received a great welcome and were told that the Japanese had left Rangoon two nights earlier. Realizing that the invasion, if carried out at full scale, would do considerable and unnecessary damage to the city, Saunders walked on to the docks, commandeered a *sampan* and sailed down the

Rangoon River to meet the invasion force, which he did on 3 May.

Seldom, if ever, can two men – and airmen at that – have been first into a city about to be attacked and captured!

For Ras Pagani's party, the dramatic change in their fortunes and their escape from all dangers was traumatic and, at first, bewildering, but their dominant feeling was one of overwhelming elation.

The Indian troops with the convoy fed them and then drove them for about an hour to an airfield where they emplaned in Dakotas which had brought in supplies for 14th Army. They were flown to Poona in India, put straight into hospital for medical checks and treatment, and issued with uniforms, someone producing a Reconnaissance Corps cap badge for Ras.

He got an Indian photographer to take his photograph in uniform and enclosed it in an airmail letter to his wife, Pip. Due to his escapes and change of name he had received no letters from her for over three years. Pip had heard nothing from him since before the fall of Singapore and did not know whether he was alive or dead.

While he was in hospital the initial euphoria of freedom evaporated – or he took it for granted – and he felt utterly deflated and impatient at his confinement in hospital when there was nothing wrong with him. He was interrogated by Intelligence officers and he urged them to fly him back to the Karenni States, where he had influence because of his service under Seagrim, to persuade the Karens to hand in their arms. If they did not, he prophesied, there would be endless trouble between the Burmese and the Karens and the latter would never again enjoy their peaceful style of life. (His real reason for this request was that he was bored and wanted action; he felt, like Seagrim, that he was an 'honorary Karen' and he wanted to see them again at this moment of victory over the hated Japanese.)

But the officers refused to take his request seriously and said that he would soon be sent home.*

His irritation at his failure to go back to the Karens was soon dispelled when he got a letter from Pip, full of joy at the news of his release and telling him that he now had a three-year-old daughter who had been born nine months after his embarkation leave in October, 1941.

A few days later he was pronounced fit, put into another Dakota and flown to England. It was not a comfortable journey but, after all the discomforts he had suffered during his life under the Japanese, he felt, philosophically, that a third-class ride was better than a first-class walk.

On landing in England he was immediately sent on leave. As the train bore him to Colchester, where Pip was living, he pushed the past into the back of his mind and began to grapple with the problem of getting to know his young family from whom he had been completely cut off for four long years.

It was going to be no easy task.

On Saturday, 29 June, 1985, Ras and Pip stood on the village green at Whissonsett. Ras, now portly, often ill and suffering from a bad heart, and still carrying the scars of those terrible wounds inflicted on him by the Burmese, stood erect like the soldier he had been in those days.

---

* They probably knew, which Ras did not, that by the end of the war over 12,000 Karens had been armed and had been fighting under the command of officers of Force 136 against the retreating Japanese, with a devastating effect.

The occasion marked the unveiling of the village sign, a tribute to Whissonsett's most famous sons, Derek and Hugh Seagrim, as it depicted both of them in uniform. The two brothers had won their Country's highest awards; Derek, the Victoria Cross, awarded for his inspiring leadership of his battalion, 7th Green Howards, on the Mareth Line in Tunisia in 1943, and Hugh, the George Cross, for his work with the Karen resistance movement in Burma and his ultimate self-sacrifice in an effort to save the Karens from wholesale massacres by the Japanese.

Neither brother had lived to know of their awards but their inspiration had lived on in the hearts of many men long after the Seagrims were dead.

Ras and Pip were guests of the Seagrim family and, as he was the only surviving Englishman to have fought the Japanese under Hugh Seagrim's command, he was asked to speak of Hugh at the ceremony.

He told the assembled villagers and guests of Hugh as he had known him in December, 1942, in the jungles of the Karenni States; a commanding officer who was also his close friend. He shared with the Karens the respect, admiration and love which they had felt for Hugh Seagrim, a man who had passed into legend among the Karen people and who is remembered there to this day.

When he had spoken, Ras's thoughts went back to the last times he had seen Hugh Seagrim. First, as a lonely figure standing in a jungle clearing and raising his hand in salutation and farewell to Ras as he left to carry out Seagrim's orders, and, secondly, that fleeting glimpse of the then unknown man in the truck in Rangoon jail who had waved to him as he went to his execution, and who was undoubtedly Hugh Seagrim.

Now, in this quiet Norfolk village where Hugh had grown up, Ras felt a mixture of pride and sadness but also gratitude that he had been privileged to have been Hugh's friend in those dangerous days.

Hugh Seagrim had inspired him, as he had inspired the Karens; it was something he would never lose and it had made him a better man.

APPENDIX A

The Aftermath

Ras Pagani, having used up eight and a half of his nine lives and been returned safely to his family, must take a back seat for a moment while we look at what happened to some of those who took part in his story.

Major D. P. Apthorp survived the war, was awarded the MBE for his work on the escape line to Sumatra and for his care of his men in the PoW camps, and died suddenly on 17 October 1983. Before his death he had begun an account of the British (Sumatra) Battalion. His widow, Ann, with the help of some who had been PoWs with her husband on the Burma-Siam railway, courageously completed the manuscript and is now offering it to publishers.

Father Paul Gaston Loizeau was aged 67 years when the Japanese occupied Papun on 22 February, 1943. Apart from a year's rest in France in 1936/37, he had been in Burma continuously since 1900. The Japanese placed him under house-arrest in Papun; he was allowed virtually no contact with the Karens, nor was he allowed to write anything, even to his Bishop, until after his release by 14th Army in July, 1945.

Late in July he sent to his HQ in Paris reports of the Papun Mission and the Karenni States during the Japanese occupation of Burma. The following year he began the slow reconstruction of Papun but never completed it. Worn out by attacks of malaria which had plagued him for thirty years, saddened because the war had destroyed so much of his life's work and had brought death and misery to his Karen flock, this good man died in Papun on 19 May, 1950, aged 74.

Father Jean Edouard Calmon, whom the Japanese, rightly, suspected of being actively involved with Seagrim and the Levies and had offered a reward for his capture, surrendered himself on 17 March, 1943, in order to prevent reprisals threatened against the Karens if he did not surrender.

He was taken to the *Kempeitai* at Thaton on 26 March but was released a week later, apparently as an inducement to persuade him to bring the Karens onto the Japanese side. This he refused to do but, according to Morrison, wrote the *Kempeitai* a long paper in which he suggested that no peace would come to the Karenni States unless the Burmese administration were removed and replaced by an all-Karen administration. But his refusal to go further in assisting them led to his re-arrest and, after several weeks of ill-treatment, he was sent to a concentration camp at Tavoy where he remained until our forces released him on 10 September, 1945.

Refusing an air passage to France, offered by 14th Army, he returned to Papun and, after Father Loizeau's death, took charge of the Papun Mission and painstakingly continued the rebuilding of Papun which Father Loizeau had begun during the last years of his life.

But it was to be to no avail; a state of armed and open

rebellion had been building up between the Karenni States and the Burmese Government since 1949 and, for nearly four years after that, Father Calmon was cut off from all contact with his Bishop in Rangoon and, indeed, with the outside world. This came to a head on 19 December, 1953, when the Burmese Air Force bombed Papun, destroying it once again and killing and wounding many Karens.

After ten years of living under conditions of war, a man of less determination than Father Calmon might have been forgiven for giving up the Papun Mission as a hopeless task, but he stuck to his post, comforted his flock and continued to expand his Mission in outlying areas.

A Father Séguinotte, of the Pères de Bétharram de la Mission de Chieng-Mai in Thailand, came to see him to ask for help in establishing a Mission. Father Calmon not only helped by translating much religious material into the Karen language but also trained two Karen priests who later went to serve these expatriate Karens at Chieng-Mai.

But, as happened with Father Loizeau, the work of running and expanding his Mission under the strains of war, wore out Father Calmon and, in 1958, he had to return to France for a rest. The people of his native village, Gramat, in the province of Lot, received him with open arms. To them he was already known as 'the dead man of 1943' because they were certain that he had been killed by the Japanese during the war.

Much refreshed, he returned to Papun in 1959 and carried on his work until 1968, in a slightly improved political atmosphere. But, in 1968, he developed haemophilia and, after two years in Rangoon hospital, he bowed to the insistence of his doctors that he should return to France for good.

It was a wrench for him to leave the Karens to whom he had devoted his life through so many dangerous years, but he realized that it was inevitable. On his return to Gramat he continued to work for the Church there and was much loved by the people.

It seems a just and fitting reward that this gallant man of God, who had served a foreign people so well in turbulent times, should die peacefully in his sleep in his home on 4 October, 1981, aged 75 years.

Ras Pagani recently visited his twin brother, Louis, at Gramat where he was received with great friendliness by the Calmon family. But he will always regret that, on his frequent journeys in France over the past twenty years, he did not know that Father Calmon had survived to return to Gramat.

For information about the fate of Seagrim, the Levies and many Karen elders, we must turn again to Ian Morrison's *Grandfather Longlegs*.

When Ras Pagani had set out for India from Pyagawpu at the beginning of March 1943, guided by old Saw Ji Bu, the elephant man who had so often guided Seagrim through the jungle, Seagrim was in hiding in the mountainous jungle region near the village of Payasedo, twenty miles west of Papun. He remained there for the next few months while the Japanese hunted for him.

By the end of March Father Calmon had surrendered and Saw Darlington had been arrested and taken to Rangoon. With Father Loizeau under house-arrest, Seagrim unable to influence the Levies and Pagani gone, the core of the resistance movement in the Papun area had disintegrated. But, in the summer, Seagrim was joined by an intelligent Karen, Saw Po Hla, whom he used, as had Pagani earlier, to collect information in the areas occupied by the Japanese. Then, in October, after several abortive sorties, Lieutenant Ba Gyaw was parachuted in to him from India, followed shortly by Major Nimmo, who had worked in the area in peacetime and knew it well. They were followed in December by Captain McCrindle and Thet Wa who brought a radio transmitter.

Now they were in regular communication with Army HQ in India but the unarmed Hudson aircraft were unsuitable for parachute drops in the mountainous jungle regions, so far from their base, especially in bad weather, and it was not possible to fulfil Seagrim's requests for arms at this time.

However, he had built up a good intelligence network and was able to give Army HQ worthwhile targets, many of which were successfully bombed. At Saw Po Hla's suggestion, Seagrim stressed that the New Law Courts in Rangoon should not be bombed as many Karens were held there by the *Kempeitai*.

Seagrim had many visitors at this time; Ta Roe, Saw Henry, an ex-policeman who was an excellent collector of information; and Saw Willie Saw who came to see him on Christmas Day, 1943, near Chawido. Everything seemed to be going very well but it was not to last much longer.

In January, 1944, the search for Seagrim was handed over exclusively to the *Kempeitai* who proceeded to terrorize the Karen villagers. Seagrim retired to a safe hide near Komupwado, ten miles south-east of Pyagawpu, but the *Kempeitai* suspected that Saw Po Hla was connected with Seagrim and arrested his family. At Seagrim's suggestion Saw Po Hla surrendered to the Japanese, denied that he had been with Seagrim and gave them such a convincing story that they released his family although they held on to him.

On 13 February, 1944, Captain Motoiche Inoue of the Rangoon *Kempeitai* came to Pyagawpu and arrested Ta Roe and some elders. By use of torture he found out that Seagrim was at Komupwado but when he rushed the camp he found, to his fury, that Seagrim had left shortly before his arrival. However, Inoue's luck was in; on his way back to Pyagawpu the next day he caught a young Karen who was acting as look-out for Seagrim and was carrying a revolver. He tortured the man until he agreed to lead them to Seagrim's new hideout.

Inoue attacked the camp, killing McCrindle and losing one of his men who McCrindle had shot. The next day Major Nimmo's camp was attacked; he also was killed and one of his men, Saw Pe, was captured.

Seagrim had escaped into the jungle when McCrindle had been killed and one of his Karens, Pa Ah, who had a married sister at Mewado, took him there. But, as a result of their systematic torturing of Karen villagers, the *Kempeitai* soon learned that Pa Ah was with Seagrim so they threatened to kill his family. Pa Ah cooked up a similar story to that given by Po Hla and moved to Pyagawpu where he gave himself up, denying vigorously that he had been with Seagrim and this appeared to satisfy the Japanese, although they kept him in custody for the time being.

By now, apart from those Karens close to Seagrim, most Karens had not seen him for a year and many were convinced that he had died of starvation or been killed by wild animals in the jungle. They expressed these convictions to the Japanese who questioned them but the latter said they would believe them only if they produced Seagrim's body. (One of the parachutists had had the ingenious idea of asking Army HQ to parachute in 'a tall

English corpse' which could then be 'found' and delivered to the Japanese. But, owing to the great difficulties of making air-drops as already related, nothing came of this scheme.)

Meanwhile Pa Ah had been imprisoned in Kyaukki, where Karen prisoners were brutally tortured by the *Kempeitai*. Also there was the young Karen who had been tortured until he had led the *Kempeitai* to Seagrim's camp near Komupwado. He made friends with Pa Ah who rashly confided to him that Seagrim was safely hidden near Mewado, never dreaming that the youth had been 'turned' and was now a *Kempeitai* informer. The man reported this information to Inoue who went straight to Mewado and threatened to imprison all Karens there unless Seagrim gave himself up.

When Seagrim heard of this he decided that he must spare these innocent Karens any further suffering on his behalf so he came out of the jungle and surrendered to Inoue in March, 1944. From there he was taken to the New Law Courts in Rangoon.

There is no evidence that he was tortured to the same extent as was Pagani, but any Karens suspected of being connected with him certainly were. It seems that the Japanese, even the *Kempeitai*, respected his courage and were also hopeful that they might persuade him to use his influence with the Karens to co-operate with the Japanese. This he refused to do.

Later he was moved to the cells in Rangoon jail and, on 2 September 1944, was court-martialled and condemned to death. Taking all the blame on himself, he made a final plea for the release of the Karens but this fell on deaf ears. Later that day he and seven others were taken by truck to Kemmendine Cemetery where they were shot.

His execution was one more example of the treachery, deceit and hypocrisy so often shown by the Japanese. Seagrim had surrendered voluntarily to save the Karens from further ill-treatment. He had been given an assurance that he would be treated as a prisoner of war and that persecution of the Karens would cease after his surrender. For all their lip-service to courage and '*bushido*' (chivalry), they usually behaved like this and it stained the honour of their Armed Forces, earning them the contempt and loathing of all decent men.

Needless to say, they also continued to terrorize the Karens until all resistance was finally crushed through fear of reprisals against innocent people. But in 1945 they were to pay a terrible price for their broken promises when the Karens, newly-armed, fell upon their weary forces as they tried to retreat from Burma to Siam and slaughtered them without mercy.

Executed with Seagrim were seven Karens including Pagani's old friend, Ah Din, and Lieutenant Ba Gyaw. Saw Po Hla, Ta Roe, Saw Digay, Saw Henry and six others were sentenced to eight years' hard labour.

Po Hla, Henry, Digay and Thet Wa later escaped from the Japanese when being moved or when on working parties. Saw Darlington, who had been arrested in 1943, was released in time to join the new Karen resistance movement in 1945. The fate of Pagani's faithful henchman, Lance Naik Mura, is not known. He told Ras that he would return to the Karenni States and rejoin the Karen Levies. One hopes that he was successful and was able to exact revenge for the tortures which he and Ras had suffered at the hands of the Japanese, and that he lived to return to his home in Assam. His loyalty to Ras was something which the latter can never forget.

Poor Pa Ah, who never forgave himself for having inadvertently betrayed Seagrim in Kyaukki, died of dysentery and, perhaps, a broken heart. Ohn Gyaw, who had insisted on giving himself up with Seagrim instead of staying in the jungle, also died of dysentery, as did many others in those filthy *Kempeitai* cells.

Ta Roe and Saw Willie Saw, and others who survived their torments, were released by our forces in 1945. They were in very poor shape but slowly recovered their health.

Of that shadowy figure who was so influential in the resistance movement, the cultured Anglophile, Saw Po Thin, we know nothing. Morrison would surely have mentioned so important a man had he been killed or imprisoned by the Japanese. Perhaps we can hope that he and his charming daughter never aroused the suspicions of the *Kempeitai* throughout those dangerous years.

Captain Inoue of the *Kempeitai* was arrested and charged with war crimes against the Karens. His fate is not known.

But, as we have seen in Chapter Twelve, Seagrim and those Karens who died or suffered incarceration, had lit a flame which did not go out.

Ras Pagani, after his miraculous survival, was discharged from the Army in the rank of Corporal, with a 25% disability pension. (The Army had, until his discharge, honoured the rank of sergeant to which Seagrim had promoted him). He disputed his discharge because he felt he was fit enough to continue his service as a regular soldier, but to no avail.

Soon after his return, Ian Morrison, having found that Ras had not been killed on the Irrawaddy, got in touch with him and added a précis of his experiences to

Grandfather Longlegs. He also wanted to write Pagani's story but Ras was too busy at that time to deal with it. In September, 1950, Ian Morrison and Christopher Buckley, war correspondents for the *Times* and *Telegraph* respectively, were killed in Korea when their Jeep ran over a land mine, so the Pagani story was still-born.

In 1946 a Military Medal arrived through the post; no citation was sent with the award nor was any suggestion made that it might be officially presented to him on some suitable occasion. This angered him; he felt that all his efforts and sufferings during the war merited some form of official presentation of the medal and, when the authorities then terminated his disability pension at short notice, he protested that they could not have it both ways – either he was fit enough to re-enlist or they should continue the pension because he was not fit.

He won the day and was allowed to re-enlist, 'in view of his good war record', but in the Royal Artillery. He was sent to Carlisle where he became driver to the Brigadier. Shortly after Pagani's arrival the latter was posted to the British Military Mission in Rangoon and he asked Ras if he would like to go with him. Ras jumped at the idea and his name was submitted to the Burmese Government.

But his application was firmly turned down. No reason was given but it seemed that the name 'Pagani' was still remembered in connection with the Karens and, as the Karens were at loggerheads with the Burmese Government at this time, Pagani was definitely '*persona non grata*'.

To ease the disappointment Ras felt at this refusal the Brigadier arranged for him to return to the infantry, first to The Royal Sussex Regiment with whom he went to Suez, and then back to his regiment, The East Surrey Regiment, in Germany where he became Motor Transport sergeant.

In January, 1959, he retired from the Army and started up a taxi service and, later, garages in Colchester and Clacton-on-Sea. By a strange chance one of his first taxi customers in Colchester was Major Apthorp whom he had not seen since he left 18 Km camp in 1942.

As he looks back over those years of strife and suffering in Burma, what are his feelings? He has a justified pride in his escapes, especially from the Burma-Siam railway, from which he made the only successful escape. He still has a contempt and loathing for the Japanese, not only on account of their treatment of him and his comrades, but also for their execution of Seagrim and their brutal persecution of the Karens. He still loves the Karen people, regarding himself as 'an honorary Karen' because he fought alongside them against the Japanese and Burmese, and their struggle, after the war, to gain independence from the Burmese Government had his full sympathy.

He attributes his survival both to his upbringing in the Convent of St Joseph, where he was taught self-reliance, and to The East Surrey Regiment who turned him from a boy into a man, trained him to be a competent soldier and also taught him both discipline and self-discipline.

But even these would not have been enough in themselves to ensure his survival under such terrible circumstances unless he had also had inspiration. That was given to him by Hugh Seagrim who had the great gift of inspiring men of different races to be courageous and to live in a spirit of self-sacrifice.

Ras Pagani owes no other man a greater debt.

APPENDIX B

National Army Museum
Royal Hospital Road
London SW3 4HT
Telephone 01–730 0717 Ext 44

From the Director
William Reid

R Pagani Esq MM
Albion
London Road
Lt Clacton
Clacton-on-Sea
Essex   26 February 1986

I enclose a copy of your citation. It was sent to me this morning by Brigadier Ryder of the Military Secretary's office at Stanmore. It does not seem to settle the question of who put you up for your Military Medal but that you earned it for three hard years. I have asked the brigadier to tell me whether there is a signature on the citation and will let you know if he tells me more.

With every good wish.

1A

820870 Cpl. PAGANI, Roy Anthony Stephen, 18 Recce Regt. 18 Div.

Following his capture at the capitulation of SINGAPORE on 15 February 1942, PAGANI first attempted to escape to SUMATRA by sampan. After twelve days he reached RENGAT, where he was transported by the Dutch Army to PADANG. PAGANI remained there for two weeks waiting to be evacuated, but on 17 March 1942 the town was handed over to the enemy and he was taken prisoner.

On 18 September 1942, while working on the Burma-Thailand railway near AMHERST, PAGANI escaped into the jungle and travelled North, disguised as a Burman and receiving some help from the local inhabitants. After eight days he was joined by an Indian who offered to lead him to a British Army Officer working in the jungle. He travelled with an escort for eleven days to a place South of MAWCHI where he met the British Major (later captured and executed in INSEIN Jail, RANGOON by the Japanese) who offered him the command of the Southern Area of his guerrilla forces. PAGANI and his partisans, operating from KADAINGTI on the YUN-ZALIN River, made many raids on enemy patrols, villages and convoys, successfully destroying much transport. He was only in contact with his commander by occasional runners.

On 9 April 1943, PAGANI was sent on a mission to contact the Allied forces at PROME, a journey which entailed crossing the PEGUYOMAS mountains, the

SALWEEN and the IRRAWADDY. He was once captured by hostile villagers and successfully got away, but later he was caught again, and was too severely wounded to make any further attempt to escape. He was handed over to the Japanese, having been free for eight months.

He was liberated by the 14th Army South of PEGU on 28 April, 1945.

APPENDIX C

Chronology

The passage of over forty years renders dates unreliable unless events were recorded at the time they occurred. I have, therefore, avoided giving dates except where events were dated by more than one source.

Major Apthorp buried his diary for that period when he left Burma early in 1944. He did not get the chance of recovering this after the war so had to rewrite that period from memory when he got home, three years after the events took place.

Father Loizeau, because of the restrictions placed on him by the Japanese from 1943–1945, also wrote his reports from memory after the war, two years after the events had occurred.

Ian Morrison was not in the Karenni States until late 1945 and his evidence was gathered from Karens, Burmans and Japanese who, although they were living there throughout those years, had to rely on their memories of events.

Ras Pagani had no diary and only a rough idea of dates, although his memory of the sequence and duration of events described in the book is good.

All these sources are probably about 90% accurate and, when married together, give as accurate a time-scale as is possible to obtain in the circumstances. But, apart from Ras Pagani, all those who produced accounts, even from memory, are now dead so I have not been able to check their stories with them.

Hugh Seagrim left no record; Morrison and the Karens thought that Pagani had been killed in 1943; Apthorp did not know until his return to England in October, 1945, that Pagani has survived, nor did he have any knowledge of Pagani's exploits after he left 18 Km Camp.

I have ignored the dates given in the citation for Pagani's Military Medal (see Appendix B). They must have originated from the Intelligence Officers who debriefed Pagani in Poona after his release. But he had little idea of dates of events when he was in the Karenni States, had spent months under terrible circumstances in Japanese hands, and was being asked to give dates of events which had taken place over two years previously. It is no wonder that there were errors.

All other evidence points to his escape from 18 Km camp in mid-November, 1942, not 18 September as stated, and his account of leaving the Karenni States, when tied to Morrison's and Father Loizeau's accounts, puts that date in the first half of March, 1943, and not 9 April as given.

Furthermore, the citation contains other inaccuracies. For instance, there was no question of Pagani 'destroying much transport' because the area in which he operated was impassable to motor vehicles and on only a few main tracks could bullock carts move. Nor were there any 'Allied Forces in Prome' – or within hundreds of miles of it

– in April, 1943. The town was recaptured by 14th Army in May, 1945.

However, these errors in no way detract from Pagani's achievements. Certainly he and his Levies killed many Japanese, BIA and hostile Burmans but, in my opinion, his outstanding achievements were:

a) his well-planned, daring and successful escape from the Burma-Siam railway where a dozen or so Australians and Dutch troops had already been shot for attempting escape,

b) his assertion of authority over the quarrelling Levies in the south,

c) his scheme of warning all villagers to take to the jungle with all their food and livestock so that visiting Japanese forces were unable to live off the country,

d) his heroic endurance of torture when in the hands of the *Kempeitai* and his refusal to be broken in spirit.

On any of these counts he earned his award many times over.

Robert Hamond

BIBLIOGRAPHY

Singapore: The Final Battle

Louis Allen *Singapore 1941–42* Davies-Poynter, London 1977

Noel Barber *Sinister Twilight* Collins, London, 1968

Capt. C. G. T. Dean MBE *The Loyal Regiment 1919–1953* Wm Brendon & Son Ltd, Mayflower Press, Watford

Frank Owen *The Fall of Singapore* Pan Illustrated

Lt Gen A. E. Percival CB, DSO, OBE, MC *The War in Malaya* Eyre & Spottiswood, London, 1949

Brigadier Ivan Simson *Singapore: Too Little, Too Late* Leo Cooper, London, 1970

Major-Gen S. Woodburn-Kirby CB, CMG, CIE, OBE, MC *Singapore: The Chain of Disaster* Cassell, London

Escapes from Singapore

Geoffrey Brooke *Alarm Starboard* Patrick Stephens Ltd, Cambridge, 1982

C. G. Gibson *The Boat* W H Allen Ltd, London

O. W. Gilmour *Singapore to Freedom* E J Burrows & Co Ltd, London, 1943

D. Russell-Roberts *Spotlight on Singapore* Anthony Gibbs & Philips, 1965

A. V. Sellwood *Stand by to Die* New English Library Ltd, 1961

Ian Skidmore *Escape from the Rising Sun* Leo Cooper, London, 1973

Rt Hon Sir John Smyth Bt, VC, MC *The Will to Live* Cassell, London, 1970

BURMA

Louis Allen *Sittang; The Last Battle* Arrow Books Ltd, London, 1976 *Burma: The Longest War 1941–45* J M Dent & Sons Ltd, London, 1984

John Bowen *Undercover in the Jungle*, William Kimber, 1978

Pat Carmichael *Mountain Battery*, Devin Books, Bournemouth, 1983

M. R. D. Foot & J. M. Langley *MI 9: Escape and Evasion 1939–45* Bodley Head, London 1979

Lionel Hudson *The Rats of Rangoon*, Leo Cooper, 1987

James Lunt *A Hell of a Licking: The Retreat from Burma 1941/42* Collins, London, 1986

Ian Morrison *Grandfather Longlegs* Faber & Faber Ltd, London, 1947

Rohan D. Rivett *Behind Bamboo* Angus & Robertson Ltd, Sydney & London 1946

Unpublished Sources

Major D. P. Apthorp, MBE *POW DIARY from 1942–45*

Rev Father Paul Gaston Loizeau *Reports from Papun Mission 1942–45* Missions Étrangères de Paris

Rev Father Jean Edouard Calmon – Documents supplied
by his twin brother, M. Louis Calmon

ACKNOWLEDGEMENTS

I am grateful to the following for their help during the writing of this book:

Faber and Faber Ltd., for allowing me to make extensive use of both information and photographs contained in the late Ian Morrison's *Grandfather Longlegs*, an account of the late Major Hugh Seagrim's leadership of the Karen resistance movement.

The late Major D. P. Apthorp, MBE, for helping me to trace Ras Pagani, and his widow, Ann, for agreeing to my use of information from her husband's diaries for the period prior to Pagani's escape from the Burma-Siam railway.

Lieutenant Colonel J. H. Seagrim, for vetting my account of the early life of his brother, Hugh, and for a photograph of the latter.

Father Jean Verinaud, Archiviste, Missions Étrangères de Paris, for information from the papers of the late Fathers, Paul Gaston Loizeau and Jean Edouard Calmon, together with photographs of the former, and to M. Louis Calmon for material and photographs of his brother.

The Imperial War Museum for allowing me to reproduce the drawing of a *Kempeitai* NCO and Ronald Searle for his generosity in waiving a fee for this because of our shared hardships at the hands of the Japanese.

Regimental Secretaries, The Royal Norfolk Regiment and The Queen's Regiment, the former for making available the diaries of the late Major Apthorp and the latter for extracts from the Regimental History, The East Surrey Regiment, for the years 1935–1940.

The National Army Museum for obtaining the citation for the award of the Military Medal to Pagani; and the Royal Geographical Society for providing photostats of 1942 maps of the Karenni States.

John Mitchell for drawing the maps, and Daphne Mitchell, not only for her skill in typing my manuscript but for taking such a personal interest in the story.

Leo Cooper and Tom Hartman for their helpful criticisms of my manuscript, and the former for not feeling, in the manner of Lady Bracknell, that 'to publish one of my books might be regarded as a misfortune; to publish two might look like carelessness.'

Ras Pagani, for whose courage I have unbounded admiration, for his patience with my incessant grilling of him for every detail of his early family life and escapes, and to both our wives for bearing, without complaint, the inconveniences caused to them during the writing of this book.

Robert Hamond